CONNECT with... WORDS!

GRADE 1

School Specialty
Publishing

Send all inquiries to:
School Specialty Publishing
8720 Orion Place
Columbus, OH 43240-2111

ISBN 0-7696-7431-3

2 3 4 5 6 7 8 9 10 POH 12 11 10 09 08 07

AMERICAN
EDUCATION
PUBLISHING™

Columbus, Ohio

Table of Contents

About The Book

Connect With Words is designed to help students increase their vocabulary skills with cross-curricular, grade-appropriate words and activities.

Activity Pages

Connect With Words is divided into 36 weeks, which is the average length of the school year. Each book is broken down into three-week units with a review lesson at the conclusion of each unit. The activity pages in the book focus on important words from different subject areas.

Keywords

A keyword is listed at the bottom of each activity page. This keyword is the link that connects students to the online activities via the CD, providing extra practice.

How to Use the CD

After inserting the CD into your computer, first follow the directions to register for the online activities database. Your registration is free and good for one year. After you have registered, click on the unit that your student is currently working on. Then, click on the appropriate keyword. This will take you to an online database of activities related to that keyword. You may choose to download up to 200 activities, which you may then print. Also included on the CD is a printable progress chart so your student can keep track of his or her progress through the workbook.

For further explanation of the online database, CD, or for technical help, refer to the help me file located on the CD.

Name: _____

Words That Describe

Describing words tell about people, places, and things. They can tell how things look, taste, sound, or feel.

Directions: Circle the two describing words in each sentence. The first one is done for you.

The (white) kitten is (fluffy).

Noisy squirrels ran up a tall tree.

The old book is torn.

The apple was sweet and crisp.

The bright sun is warm.

Yellow ducks swam in a little pond.

Adjectives

31

Name:_____

UNIT 2

Words That Describe

Some words describe a person, place, or thing. These words tell more about a naming word.

Example: The shoe is **old**.

Directions: Use the words in the Word Bank to write the correct describing word in each box.

| cold | round | funny | light | sad | fat |

Adjectives

32

Name:_____

Words That Describe

A **describing word** tells about a noun. It can tell what kind, what color, what size, what shape, or how many.

Directions: Use the words in the Word Bank to complete each sentence with the correct describing word.

green	big	three	round	bushy	six

1. A [beaver image] has _____ teeth.

2. A [squirrel image] has a _____ tail.

3. A [ladybug image] has _____ legs.

4. The [tadpole image] will become a _____ frog.

5. The _____ [bats image] hang by their tails.

6. An [owl image] has _____ eyes.

Name:_____

Words About Europe

Europe is the second smallest continent in the world. It is between Asia and the Atlantic Ocean. The Mediterranean Sea is to the south. Many countries and mountain chains make up the continent. One of the most famous mountain chains is the Alps.

Directions: Trace and write the words. Then, color the map of Europe.

Europe

Alps

Atlantic Ocean

sea

south

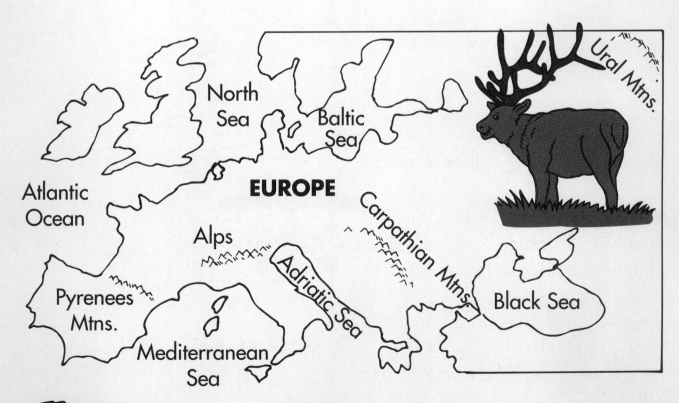

Name:_____

UNIT 2

Words About Amphibians

Directions: Use the words in the Word Bank to complete the puzzle about amphibians. Then, color only the amphibians.

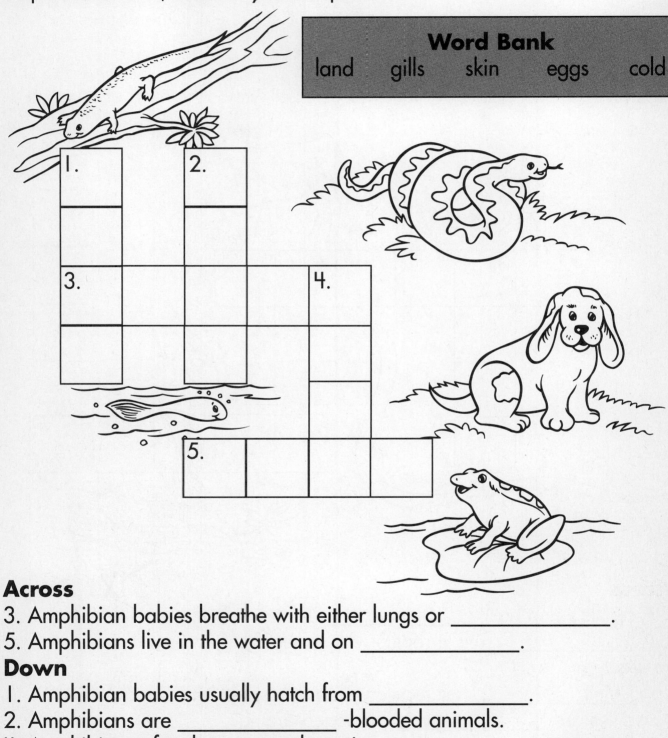

Word Bank

land   gills   skin   eggs   cold

Across

3. Amphibian babies breathe with either lungs or _____.

5. Amphibians live in the water and on _____.

Down

1. Amphibian babies usually hatch from _____.

2. Amphibians are _____ -blooded animals.

4. Amphibians often have smooth, moist _____.

 Amphibians

35

Name:_____

UNIT 2

Words About Reptiles

Directions: Use the words in the Word Bank to complete the puzzle about reptiles. Then, color only the reptiles.

Word Bank				
eggs	cold	scales	snake	turtle

Across

2. A reptile's skin has _____.

5. A _____ is a reptile with no legs.

Down

1. A _____ is a reptile with a hard shell on its back.

3. Reptiles are _____ -blooded animals.

4. Baby reptiles hatch from _____.

Reptiles

36

Name:_____

Words About Insects

Directions: Use the words in the Word Bank to complete the puzzle about insects. Then, color only the insects.

Word Bank

skeleton   legs   wings   three   eyes

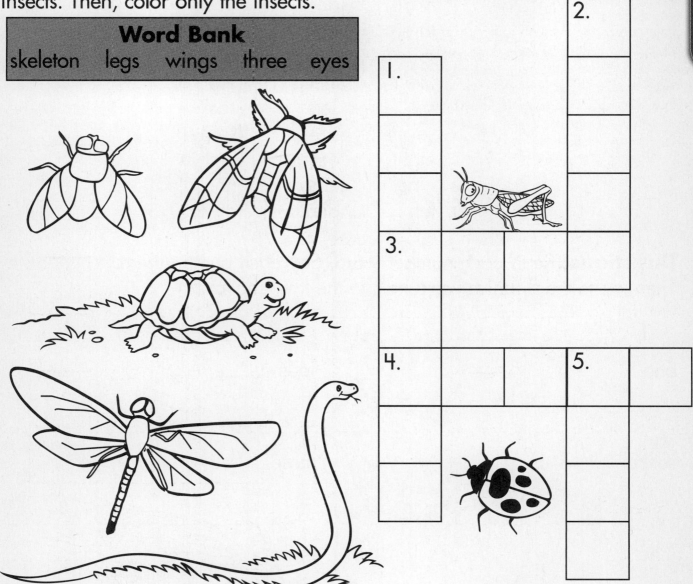

Across

3. Insects have three pairs of _____.
4. Insects have _____ main body sections.

Down

1. Insects have a hard outer _____.
2. Many insects have two pairs of _____.
5. Insects have simple and compound _____.

Name:_____

UNIT 2

Spanish Number Words

1	one	uno	(ōō-nō)
2	two	dos	(dōs)
3	three	tres	(trās)
4	four	cuatro	(kwǒ-trō)
5	five	cinco	(sēn-ko)
6	six	seis	(sās)
7	seven	siete	(sē-ě-tā)
8	eight	ocho	(ō-chō)
9	nine	nueve	(nōō-ā-vā)
10	ten	diez	(dē-ěz)

Directions: Read each number word. Say each number word in Spanish. Then, write the Spanish word next to the English word.

one _____   four _____

seven _____   three _____

nine _____   eight _____

ten _____   six _____

two _____   five _____

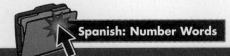

Name:_____

Words That Describe

Directions: Circle the describing word in each sentence. Draw a line from each sentence to the picture it describes.

1. The hungry dog is eating.

2. The tiny bird is flying.

3. Horses have long legs.

4. She is a fast runner.

5. The little boy was lost.

Name:_____

Words That Describe

Directions: Draw a line from each word to the picture it describes.

old

soft

hot

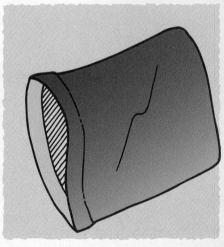

sweet

wet

tall

Adjectives

Name:_____

Words That Describe

Directions: Use the words in the Word Bank to write the correct describing word in each box.

Word Bank					
wet	round	funny	soft	sad	tall

- - - - - - - - - - - -

- - - - - - - - - - - -

- - - - - - - - - - - -

- - - - - - - - - - - -

- - - - - - - - - - - -

- - - - - - - - - - - -

Name:_____

UNIT 2

Words About Antarctica

Antarctica, the fifth largest continent, is the most southern continent. It is covered with ice and is so cold in the winter that only scientists and exploration groups live there. No animals live on the ice, but many live along the edge of the ice by the sea.

Directions: Trace and write the words. Then, color the map of Antarctica.

Antarctica

ice   cold

scientist

Pacific Ocean

Ross Sea

Weddell Sea

• South Pole

ANTARCTICA

Atlantic Ocean

Name:_____

Words About Mammals

Directions: Use the words in the Word Bank to complete the puzzle about mammals. Then, color only the mammals.

Word Bank
hair   babies   lungs   milk   warm

Across
2. A mammal's body is usually covered with _____.
3. Mother mammals feed _____ to their babies.
5. Mammal's _____ are born alive.

Down
1. Mammals are _____ -blooded.
4. Mammals breathe with _____.

Name:_____

UNIT 2

Words About Animal Young

Directions: Draw a line from each adult animal to its baby. Then, color the animals.

 hen

 chick

 pig

gosling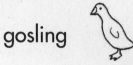

 duck

piglet

 goose

duckling

 goat

kid

 horse

foal

Name:_____

Words About Animal Young

Directions: Draw a line from each adult animal to its baby. Use the words in the Word Bank to write the correct animal name under each picture.

Word Bank			
kitten	lamb	calf	puppy

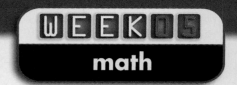

Name:_____

Spanish Number Words

Directions: Draw a line from each English number word to the correct Spanish number word.

one	tres ●●●
two	cinco ●●●●●
three	siete ●●●● ●●●
four	nueve ●●●●● ●●●●
five	uno ●
six	diez ●●●●● ●●●●●
seven	cuatro ●●●●
eight	dos ●●
nine	seis ●●● ●●●
ten	ocho ●●●● ●●●●

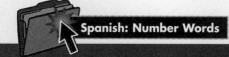

UNIT 2

Name:_____

Words That Are Adjectives

Describing words are also called **adjectives**.

Directions: Circle the describing word in each sentence.

1. The juicy apple is on the plate.

2. The furry dog is eating the bone.

3. It was a sunny day.

4. The kitten drinks warm milk.

5. The baby has a loud cry.

UNIT 2

Name:_____

Words That Are Adjectives

Directions: Draw a picture of your favorite animal. Write two sentences that tell about your picture. Make sure to use a describing word in each sentence.

UNIT 2

Name:_____

Words That Are Adjectives

Adjectives tell us more about a person, place, or thing.

Directions: Use the words in the Word Bank to write the correct adjective next to each picture.

Word Bank
happy   round   sick   cold   long

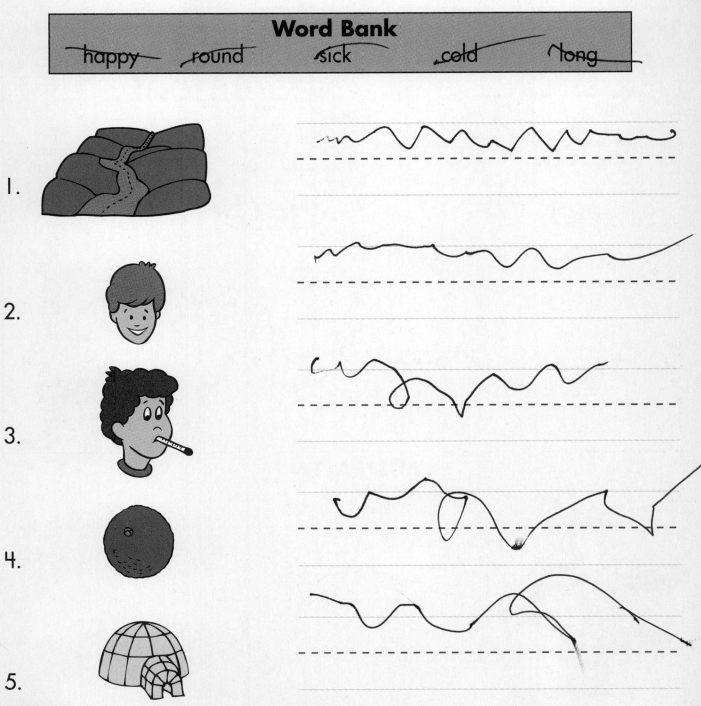

1.

2.

3.

4.

5.

Name:_____

UNIT 2

Words About Australia

Australia is the smallest continent in the world. It is an island in the South Pacific Ocean. Much of Australia is desert, so there are not many people who live there. Since Australia is so far away from the other continents, its animals look very different.

Directions: Trace the words. Then, color the map of Australia.

Australia   continent

Pacific Ocean

island   desert

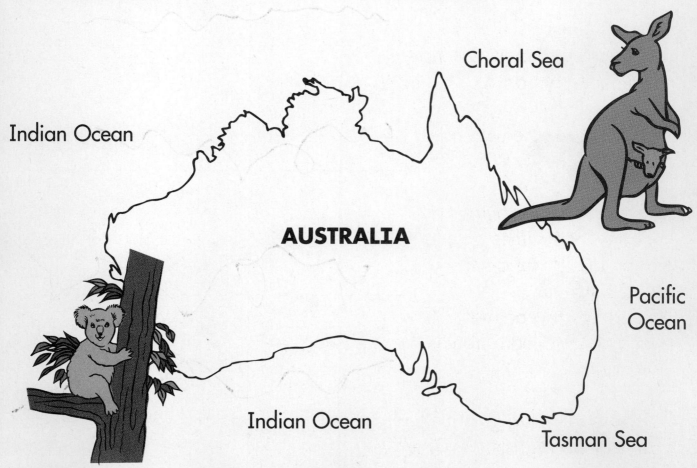

Choral Sea

Indian Ocean

AUSTRALIA

Pacific Ocean

Indian Ocean

Tasman Sea

Name:_____

Words About Zoo Animals

Directions: Write the name of the animal that answers each riddle. Use the pictures and animal words to help you.

bear

zebra

lion

camel

elephant

1. I am big and brown. I sleep all winter. What am I?

- -

2. I look like a horse with black and white stripes. What am I?

- -

3. I have one or two humps on my back. Sometimes people ride on me. What am I?

- -

4. I am a very big animal. I have a long nose called a trunk. What am I?

- -

5. I have sharp claws and teeth. I am a great big cat. What am I?

- -

Name:_____

UNIT 2

Words About Farm Animals

Directions: Read the story. Then, answer the questions.

You can hear many sounds on the farm. Roosters crow in the morning. The cows moo, and the donkeys say, "hee-haw." You might even hear the tractor motor humming.

1. What animal crows in the morning?

2. What sound does the cow make?

3. What in the story is not an animal?

4. What animals say, "hee-haw"?

Directions: Use the words in the Word Bank to find the farm words. Look up, down, and across.

donkey		a	l	b	x	m	d	y
		e	u	m	p	o	o	a
moo		k	c	f	h	o	n	j
		q	k	t	u	l	k	w
rooster		r	o	o	s	t	e	r
		c	e	n	o	s	y	v
tractor		t	r	a	c	t	o	r

Farming

52

Name:_____

Words About Zoo and Farm Animals

Directions: Read the story. Then, use the words in the Word Bank to complete the puzzle about zoo and farm animals.

The zoo is for wild animals. Tigers live at the zoo. Some snakes live at the zoo. The farm is for tame animals. Ducks and donkeys live on farms.

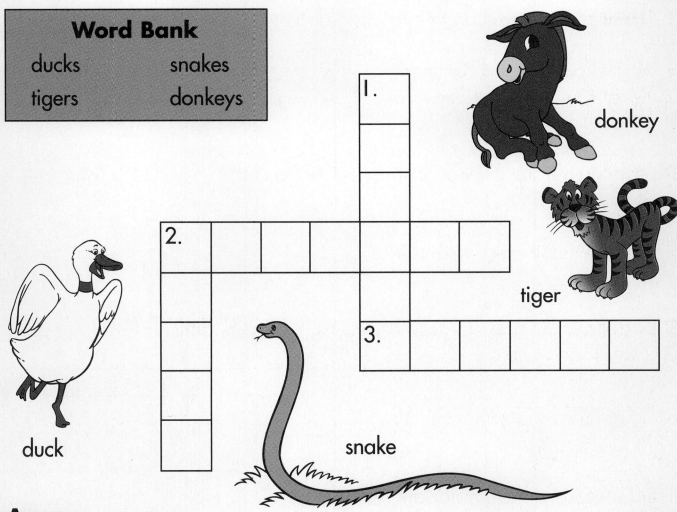

Word Bank

ducks   snakes

tigers   donkeys

donkey

tiger

duck

snake

Across
2. These animals say, "hee-haw." They live on the farm.
3. These animals are long and thin. Some live in the zoo.

Down
1. These animals have stripes. They live in the zoo.
2. These animals say, "quack." They live on the farm.

Zoo, Farming

53

© 2007 School Specialty Publishing

Name:_____

UNIT 2

Unit 2 Review

Directions: Circle the describing words in each sentence.

1. Amphibians have smooth skin.

2. A turtle has a hard shell on its back.

3. The little puppy will grow into a big dog.

4. Antarctica is a cold continent.

5. Wild animals live at the zoo.

Directions: Trace the words. Then, write the correct word to answer each question.

yes   no

1. Is Australia an island in the Atlantic Ocean? _____

2. Do mammals breathe with lungs? _____

3. Does a zebra have black and white stripes? _____

4. Is siete the Spanish word for six? _____

5. Does a cow say, "hee-haw"? _____

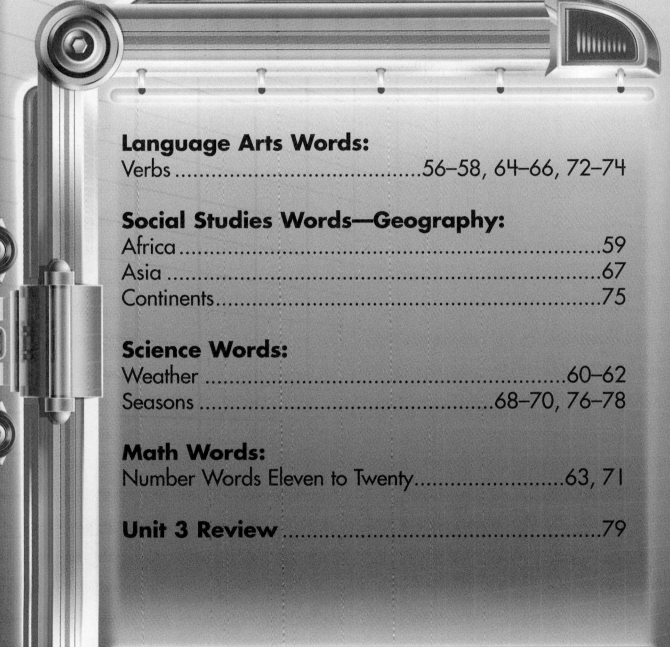

Name:_____

UNIT 3

Action Words

An **action word** tells what a person or thing can do.

Example: Fred **kicks** the ball.

Directions: Circle the action word that tells what each child is doing.

jump

boy

sleep

bed

hello

talk

skate

mittens

hop

sidewalk

sing

song

swim

deep

story

read

Verbs

56

© 2007 School Specialty Publishing

Name:_____

Action Words

Action words tell things we can do.

Directions: Trace and write the action words. The first one is done for you.

1.  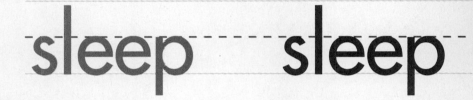 sleep   sleep

2.  run

3.  make

4.  ride

5.  play

6.  stop

Name:_____

Action Words

Directions: Underline the action word in each sentence. Then, draw a line from each sentence to the picture it describes. The first one is done for you.

The dog <u>barks</u>.

The birds fly.

A fish swims.

A monkey swings.

A turtle crawls.

A boy talks.

UNIT 3

Name:_____

Words About Africa

Africa is the second largest continent in the world. Almost all of Africa is a hot, dry desert. It is the largest desert in the world. The desert is called the Sahara. The longest river in the world, the Nile River, flows through Africa. Many big animals live in the forests of central Africa where it is hot, but plants and trees grow well because there are heavy rains.

Directions: Trace and write the words. Then, color the map of Africa.

Africa ------------------ desert ------------------

rain ------------------ river ------------------

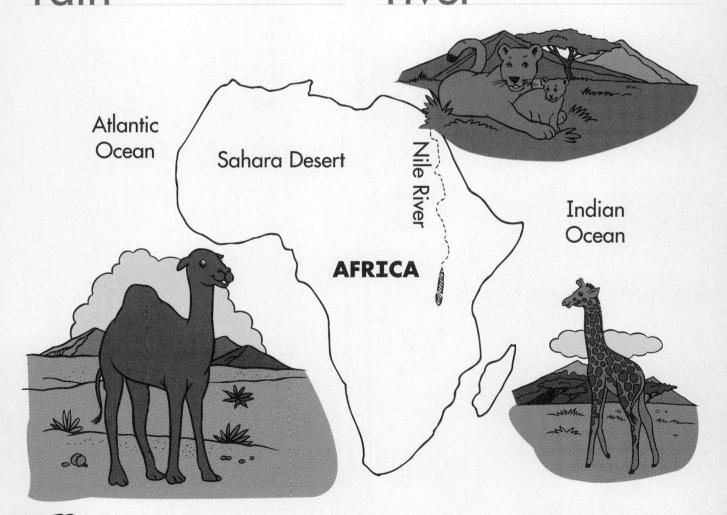

Atlantic Ocean

Sahara Desert

Nile River

AFRICA

Indian Ocean

UNIT 3

Name:_____

Weather Words

Directions: Trace and write the weather words. Then, color the pictures. The first one is done for you.

 sun   sun

 snow

 hot

rain

 wet

cold

Name: _____

Weather Words

Directions: The letters in each weather word are mixed up. Unscramble the letters and write each word correctly. The first one is done for you.

1.  nsu

sun

2. tew

3.  dcol

4. wosn

5.  tho

6. arin

61

Name:_____

Weather Words

Directions: Use the words in the Word Bank to complete each sentence with the correct weather word. Put a period at the end of the telling sentences and a question mark at the end of the asking sentences. The first one is done for you.

Word Bank			
rain	water	wet	hot

1. The sun makes me **hot** ⊙

2. When it rains, the grass gets _____ ☐

3. Do you think it will _____ on our picnic ☐

4. Should you drink the _____ from the rain ☐

UNIT 3

Name:_____

Number Words

Directions: Draw a line from each number to the correct number word.

16	fourteen
15	nineteen
14	seventeen
19	eighteen
17	fifteen
18	sixteen

Directions: Write the missing number in each group. Then, spell that number in the space below. The first one is done for you.

13, __14__, 15   9, 10, _____

fourteen   - - - - - - - - - - - - - - - -

12, _____, 14   11, _____, 13

- - - - - - - - - - - - - -   - - - - - - - - - - - - - - - - -

UNIT 3

Name:_____

Words That Are Verbs

A **verb** is an action word. A verb tells what a person or thing does.

Example: Jane **reads** a book.

Directions: Circle the verb in each sentence.

Two tiny dogs dance.

The bear climbs a ladder.

The clown falls down.

A tiger jumps through a ring.

A boy eats popcorn.

A woman swings on a trapeze.

Verbs

64

Name:_____

Words That Are Verbs

Directions: Use the words in the Word Bank to complete each sentence with the correct verb.

Word Bank					
play	jump	stop	ride	make	run

One day, Mom said I could _____ the school bus home

with Pat. We watched Pat's

with a  . Then, Pat told me, "My mother said she would

_____ some 🍪🍪 . I'll get us some."

Pat went inside to get the 🍪🍪 . Just then, I saw a

_____ into the yard. Oh, no! He might chase Pat's

 . I had to _____ him!

Pat came back with the 🍪🍪 . The  began to

_____ on Pat and lick Pat's face. Then, he ran off with

the 🍪🍪 .

 **Verbs**

Name:_____

Words That Are Verbs

Directions: Use the words in the Word Bank to write five sentences. Use a different verb for each sentence.

Word Bank				
catch	color	eat	grow	fly

1. _____

_____

2. _____

_____

3. _____

_____

4. _____

_____

5. _____

Name: _____

Words About Asia

Asia is the world's largest continent. More than one-half of all the people in the world live in Asia. Asia contains Russia, which is the largest country in the world. China, the country that is home to the most people in the world, is also in Asia. The tallest mountains in the world are in India, a country that is in Asia.

Directions: Trace and write the words. Then, color the map of Asia.

Asia   Russia

China   India

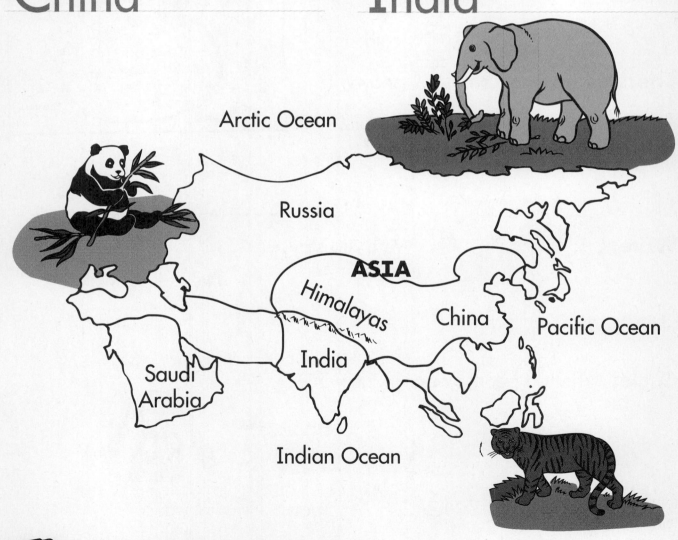

Arctic Ocean

Russia

ASIA

Himalayas

China   Pacific Ocean

India

Saudi
Arabia

Indian Ocean

Name:_____

Winter Words

Directions: Read about winter. Look at the picture. Then, complete the activities. There may be more than one correct answer.

Winter can be cold and snowy. Animals stay near each other to stay warm. People wear coats, hats, and gloves. Children make snowmen. It is fun to play in the snow.

Check: Winter can be: 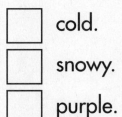 cold.
snowy.
purple.

Write:  We try to stay _____.

like   warm

Circle: What do people wear in the winter?

gloves   hat   pan   coat

Name:_____

Spring Words

Directions: Read about spring. Look at the picture. Then, complete the activities. There may be more than one correct answer.

It is warm in the spring. Flowers begin to bloom. Trees have new leaves. Birds make their nests and lay eggs.

_____

- - - - - - - - - - - - - - - - - -

Write: It is _____ in the spring.

                warm   last

Circle: What can you see in the spring?

Check: What do birds do in the spring?

☐ Birds make nests.

☐ They lay eggs.

☐ They wash dishes.

UNIT 3

Name:_____

Summer Words

Directions: Read about summer. Look at the picture. Then, complete the activities. There may be more than one correct answer.

Summer can be very hot. It is the time when children are out of school. They have fun playing with friends, swimming to stay cool, and sometimes going on family picnics and vacations.

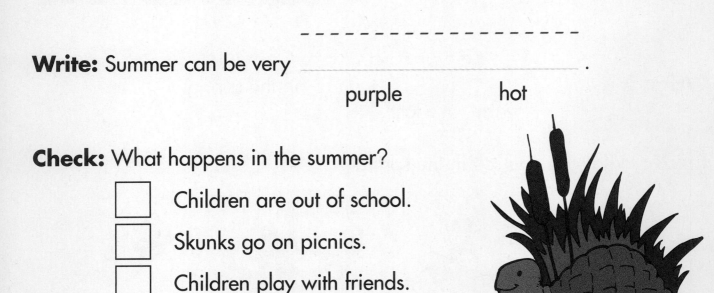

_____
_ _ _ _ _ _ _ _ _ _ _ _ _ _ _ _ _ _

Write: Summer can be very _____ .

purple   hot

Check: What happens in the summer?

☐ Children are out of school.

☐ Skunks go on picnics.

☐ Children play with friends.

Write: What do you like to do in the summer?

_____
_ _
_____

Name:_____

Number Words

Directions: Trace and write the number words. Then, color the numbers.

11 — eleven — — — — — — — — — — —

12 — twelve — — — — — — — — — — —

13 — thirteen — — — — — — — — — —

14 — fourteen — — — — — — — — — —

15 — fifteen — — — — — — — — — —

16 — sixteen — — — — — — — — — —

17 — seventeen — — — — — — — — —

18 — eighteen — — — — — — — — —

19 — nineteen — — — — — — — — —

20 — twenty — — — — — — — — — —

Name:_____

UNIT 3

Words That Are Verbs

The words **is**, **are**, and **am** are special verbs.

Use **is** to tell about one person or thing.
Use **are** to tell about more than one thing.
Use **are** with the word you.
Use **am** with the word I.

Directions: Write **is**, **are**, or **am** to complete each sentence.

1. The lake _____ deep.

2. Many fish _____ under the water.

3. I _____ at the lake.

4. Sally _____ with me.

5. We _____ busy catching fish.

6. You _____ welcome to join us.

Name:_____

Words That Are Verbs

Use **is** in sentences about one person or one thing. Use **are** in sentences about more than one person or thing.

Example: The dog **is** barking.
The dogs **are** barking.

Directions: Write **is** or **are** to complete each sentence.

1. Jim _____ playing baseball.

2. Fred and Sam _____ good friends.

3. Cupcakes _____ my favorite treat.

4. Lisa _____ a good soccer player.

Verbs

73

© 2007 School Specialty Publishing

UNIT 3

Name:_____

Words That Are Verbs

Directions: Write **is** or **are** to complete each sentence.

1. Cats and dogs _____ good pets.

2. Bill _____ my best friend.

3. Apples _____ good to eat.

4. Pedro _____ coming to my house.

5. We _____ going to the zoo.

6. When _____ you all going to the zoo?

Name:_____

Words About the Continents

Directions: The letters in each word are mixed up. Unscramble the letters and write the name of each continent correctly. Use the Word Bank to help you.

Word Bank			
Africa	Australia	North America	Antarctica
	Asia	Europe	South America

1. rtonh miecara _____

2. cfiara _____

3. eropeu _____

4. uhots ecaamir _____

5. saia _____

6. tnrtaiacac _____

7. asurilaat _____

Geography

75

© 2007 School Specialty Publishing

Name:_____

UNIT 3

Autumn Words

Directions: Read about autumn. Look at the picture. Then, complete the activities. There may be more than one correct answer.

The air gets cool in the autumn. Children go back to school. Animals store food for the winter. Leaves turn red, yellow, and orange. It is a pretty time of the year.

_____

- - - - - - - - - - - - - - - - - - -

Write: The air gets _____ in the autumn.

            time   cool

Check: What happens in the autumn?

☐ Children go back to school.

☐ Animals store food.

☐ The air is very hot.

Color:

 red   yellow   orange

Name:_____

Autumn Words

Directions: Read about raking leaves. Then, answer the questions.

I like to rake leaves. Do you? Leaves die each year. They get brown and dry. They fall from the trees. Then, people rake them up.

1. What color are leaves when they die?

_____

_ _ _ _ _ _ _ _ _ _ _ _ _ _ _ _

_____

_ _ _ _ _ _ _ _ _ _ _ _ _ _ _ _

2. What happens when they die?

_____

_ _ _ _ _ _ _ _ _ _ _ _ _ _ _ _

_____

_ _ _ _ _ _ _ _ _ _ _ _ _ _ _ _

3. What do people do when leaves fall?

_____

_ _ _ _ _ _ _ _ _ _ _ _ _ _ _ _

_____

Seasons

Name:_____

Words About Seasons

Directions:

1. Use the words in the Word Bank to write the correct season under each picture.
2. Color the clothes for autumn blue.
3. Color the clothes for winter red.
4. Color the clothes for spring green.
5. Color the clothes for summer yellow.

Word Bank	
Spring	Summer
Autumn	Winter

- - - - - - - - - - - - - - - - - -

- - - - - - - - - - - - - - - - - -

- - - - - - - - - - - - - - - - - -

- - - - - - - - - - - - - - - - - -

Name:_____

Unit 3 Review

Directions: Use the words in the Word Bank to complete each sentence.

Word Bank							
snow	are	China	desert	flows	jump	fly	sixteen

1. I like to _____ in the autumn leaves.

2. The number _____ comes after fifteen.

3. The Sahara is the largest _____ in the world.

4. The Nile River _____ through Africa.

5. There _____ seven continents in the world.

6. Our town gets a lot of _____ in the winter.

7. Russia, _____, and India are all part of Asia.

8. My family will _____ to Australia for our summer vacation.

UNIT 4

Name:_____

Words That Are Pronouns

Sometimes we use other words to name people. For a boy or a man, we use **he**. For a girl or a woman, we use **she**. For two or more people, we use **they**. **He**, **she**, and **they** are called **pronouns**.

Directions: Write **he**, **she**, or **they** to complete each sentence. The first one is done for you.

1. The boy likes cookies.

He

likes cookies.

2. The girl is running fast.

_____

is running fast.

3. The woman has a cold.

_____

has a cold.

4. Two children came to school.

_____

came to school.

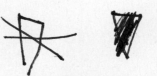

Name:_____

Words That Are Pronouns

Pronouns are words that you can use instead of nouns. **She**, **he**, **it**, and **they** are pronouns.

Directions: Read each sentence. Then, complete each sentence with the correct pronoun.

She   He   It   They

1. Dan likes funny jokes. _____ likes funny jokes.

2. Peg and Sam went to the zoo. _____ went to the zoo.

3. The dog digs in the yard. _____ likes to dig in the yard.

4. Sara is a very good dancer. _____ is a very good dancer.

5. Fred and Ed are twins. _____ are twins.

UNIT 4

Name:_____

Words That Are Pronouns

A **pronoun** is a word that can take the place of a noun in a sentence.

Example:
My dad is a pilot. **He** flies airplanes.

Directions: Circle the pronoun that can take the place of the bold words in each sentence.

1. **My mother** is a pilot, too.   They   She

2. **Mom and Dad** own a small plane.   We   They

3. **My brother** wants to be a pilot.   It   He

4. **Mother** says flying is fun.   She   He

5. **Dad** loves to fly.   They   He

6. **My brother** is older than I am.   He   We

Name:_____

Community Words

Directions: Look at the map. Use the words in the Word Bank to write the correct name under each place. Then, color the map.

Word Bank

| school | city | home | lake | pond | store |

Name:_____

Time of Day Words

Directions: Trace and write the time of day words. Then, look at each picture. Write **day** or **night** on each line to tell the time.

day
day -

night
night - - - - - - - - - - - - - - - - - - -

UNIT 4

Name:_____

Time of Day Words

Directions: Use the words in the Word Bank to write the correct time of day words under each picture.

Word Bank							
stars	sun	moon	rays	dark	light	night	day

UNIT 4

Name:_____

Space Words

Directions: Read about the night sky.
Look at the picture. Then, complete
the activities.

Do you ever look at the moon at night?
The moon travels around Earth. It gets
its light from the sun. People have gone
to the moon in spaceships. They have
walked on the moon. They even brought
back moon rocks to study.

Circle: The moon travels around   the room.

                                                     Earth.

- -

Write: The moon gets its light from _____.

                                                    Earth   the sun

Check: How did men go to the moon? ☐ spaceships
                                                              ☐ automobiles

Circle: Yes or No
            Men have walked on the moon.   Yes   No

Circle: What did men bring back from the moon?   stars

                                                                        rocks

Color: Draw a red spaceship on the moon.

Name:_____

Ordinal Number Words

Directions: Use the words in the Word Bank to write the correct ordinal number word on each line.

Word Bank				
second	fifth	seventh	first	tenth
third	eighth	sixth	fourth	ninth

1._____ 6._____

2._____ 7._____

3._____ 8._____

4._____ 9._____

5._____ 10._____

Directions: Underline the word that tells which picture is circled in each row.

1.
             fourth   sixth

2.
        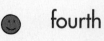   third   fifth

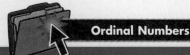

Ordinal Numbers   88   © 2007 School Specialty Publishing

Name:_____

Words That Are Articles

Articles are small words that help us better understand nouns. **A** and **an** are articles. Use **a** before a word that begins with a consonant. Use **an** before a word that begins with a vowel.

Example: We looked in **a** nest. It had **an** eagle in it.

Directions: Write **a** or **an** to complete each sentence. The first one is done for you.

I found ____a____ book. It had a story about _____ ant

in it. In the story, _____ lion gave three wishes to _____

ant. The ant's first wish was to ride _____ elephant. The second

wish was to ride _____ alligator. The last wish was

_____ wish for three more wishes.

Articles

89

© 2007 School Specialty Publishing

Name:_____

Words That Are Articles

Articles are words that come before nouns. **A** and **an** are articles. Use **a** before a word that begins with a consonant. Use **an** before a word that begins with a vowel.

Example: a peach   **an** apple

Directions: Write **a** or **an** to complete each sentence. The first one is done for you.

1. My bike had _____ **a** _____ flat tire.

2. We had _____ party for my grandfather.

3. We saw _____ lion sleeping in the shade.

4. He brought _____ blanket to the game.

5. They went to _____ orchard to pick apples.

6. He ate _____ orange for lunch.

Articles   90   © 2007 School Specialty Publishing

Name:_____

Words That Are Articles

A, **an**, and **the** are called **articles**. Use **a** when the next word begins with a consonant sound and is a single thing. Use **an** when the next word begins with a vowel sound and is a single thing.

Example: **a** chair
an antelope

The can take the place of both **a** and **an**. You can use **the** when the next word is a single thing or more than one thing.

Example: **the** beaver
the flowers

Directions: Underline the correct article for each word.

1.	(the, an)	field	11.	(a, the)	outfield
2.	(a, an)	award	12.	(the, an)	surfboard
3.	(an, the)	ball	13.	(an, the)	team
4.	(a, the)	wheels	14.	(an, the)	shin guards
5.	(a, an)	inning	15.	(a, an)	helmet
6.	(an, the)	sticks	16.	(a, an)	glove
7.	(the, a)	goalposts	17.	(the, an)	net
8.	(a, an)	obstacle	18.	(a, the)	skates
9.	(a, an)	umpire	19.	(a, the)	tennis shoes
10.	(an, the)	quarterback	20.	(a, an)	touchdown

Name: _____

Community Words

Directions: Use the words in the Word Bank to write the correct community word in each sentence.

Word Bank			
hospital	bookstore	bakery	park

1. My mom loves doughnuts. Dad and I wanted to surprise her with some. We stopped at the

   _____

   - .

2. I love to read books! My mom said she would buy me a book at the

   _____

   - .

3. I hurt my ankle at my basketball game. My coach took me to the

   _____

   - .

4. It was a warm summer day, and my family went to the

   _____

   - .

UNIT 4

Name:_____

Space Words

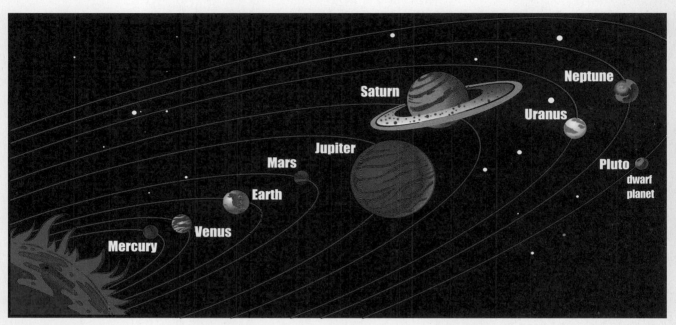

Directions: Imagine that you are traveling from the sun to outer space. Write **sun** first. Then, write the names of the planets in order.

1. _____

2. _____

3. _____

4. _____

5. _____

6. _____

7. _____

8. _____

9. _____

10. _____

Space

93

Name: _____

Space Words

Directions: Read about Earth.
Look at the picture. Then, complete the
activities. There may be more than one
correct answer.

Earth is a planet. It is the planet where
we live. Earth has land and water. It
gets light and heat from the sun. Earth
has one moon. Many people think
there is life on other planets. Earth is
the only planet that we know has life.

_____

- - - - - - - - - - - - - - - - - -

Unscramble: Earth is the _____ where we live.

l e t p n a

Check:

☐ I have land and water.
☐ I get light and heat from the sun.
☐ I have five moons.
☐ I have one moon.
☐ I am a planet.

Circle: Earth is the only planet that we know has   stars.

life.

Color: Color the picture of Earth. Draw one yellow moon in the picture.

Name:_____

Space Words

Directions: Use the words in the Word Bank to answer each riddle.

Word Bank
float
stars
Mars
sun
Earth
craters
shuttle
Saturn

1. This huge star lights the day.

_____ _____ _____

2. These shine at night.

_____ _____ _____ _____

3. These are on the moon.

_____ _____ _____ _____ _____

4. This is our home planet.

_____ _____ _____ _____

5. This flies into space.

_____ _____ _____ _____ _____ _____ _____

6. This planet is red.

_____ _____ _____ _____

7. This planet has rings.

_____ _____ _____ _____ _____ _____

8. Astronauts do this in space.

_____ _____ _____ _____

Space

95

Ordinal Number Words

Ordinal numbers show order in a series of things. **First**, **second**, and **third** are ordinal numbers.

Directions: Draw a line from each ordinal number to the correct picture.

UNIT 4

eighth

second

third

fourth

sixth

first

ninth

fifth

seventh

tenth

Name:_____

Words With Prefixes

A **prefix** is a word part that you can add to the beginning of a word to change its meaning.

Directions: Read each prefix and its meaning. Add the prefix to the root word to make a new word. Then, complete each sentence with the correct word.

Prefixes	(Meaning)	Root Word	New Word
bi	(two)	cycle	
dis	(away from)	appear	
mis	(wrong)	place	
pre	(before)	school	

1. Did you go to _____ before kindergarten?

2. The magician made the rabbit _____ .

3. Put your things where they belong so you don't _____ them.

4. Can you ride a _____ ?

UNIT 4

Name:_____

Words With Suffixes

A **suffix** is a word part that you can add to the end of a word to change its meaning.

Directions: Read each suffix and its meaning.

The suffix **ful** means "full of." **Cheerful** means "full of cheer."
The suffix **less** means "without." **Cloudless** means "without clouds."
The suffix **ness** means "a state of being." **Darkness** means "being dark."
The suffix **ly** means "in this way." **Slowly** means "in a slow way."

Directions: Add the suffixes to the words to make new words.

1. care + ful =

2. pain + less =

3. brave + ly =

4. sad + ly =

5. sick + ness =

UNIT 4

Name:_____

Words With Prefixes and Suffixes

Directions: See how many new words you can make by adding prefixes and suffixes to the root words. You can use the prefixes, suffixes, and root words as many times as you like.

Prefixes:				
bi	dis	ex	mis	pre

Root Words:				
play	obey	friend	feel	health
polite	kind	thought	cycle	like

Suffixes:			
ly	ful	ness	less

1. _____

2. _____

3. _____

4. _____

5. _____

6. _____

7. _____

8. _____

9. _____

10. _____

11. _____

12. _____

Prefixes, Suffixes

UNIT 4

Community Words

Directions: Trace the word. Then, complete each sentence with the word. Draw a picture of a house.

house house

Here is my _____ . I like my _____ .

Name:_____

Sky, Land, and Sea Words

Directions: Read the words in the Word Bank.
Draw a circle around the sky words.
Draw a line under the land words.
Draw a box around the sea words.
Then, write the correct sky, land, and sea words in each box.

Word Bank		
city	rabbit	planet
cloud	forest	whale
shark	moon	shell

Sky Words

_____   _____   _____

Land Words

_____   _____   _____

Sea Words

_____   _____   _____

UNIT 4

Name:_____

Words for Living and Nonliving Things

Directions: Read about living and nonliving things. Then, answer the questions.

tree

water

grass

turtle

flower

leaf

rock

Living things need air, food, and water.
Living things grow.
Some living things move.
Some living things do not move.

1. What is not living in the picture? _____

_____

2. Go outside. Find something living. What is it? _____

_____

3. Find something not living. What is it? _____

4. Find other things. Write them here.

Living	Nonliving

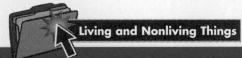
UNIT 4

Name:_____

Words for Living and Nonliving Things

Directions: Use the words on the treasure chest to write the correct things in each list.

Living	Nonliving
1.	1.
2.	2.
3.	3.
4.	4.
5.	5.
6.	6.

car
girl
hen
house
boat
dog
plane
bird
tree
cow
window
rock

Name:_____

Unit 4 Review

Directions: Draw a line to match each word or words to the correct description.

1. night   Children go here to learn.

2. sickness   People use this to go to the moon.

3. he, she, they   This shines during the day.

4. house   This belongs in the sea.

5. third   These are pronouns.

6. sun   This word has the prefix "bi."

7. a, an, the   This means "being sick."

8. spaceship   Earth is in this position from the sun.

9. school   This is when you go to bed.

10. bicycle   These are articles.

11. whale   These need air, food, and water.

12. living things   Some people live in this.

UNIT 4

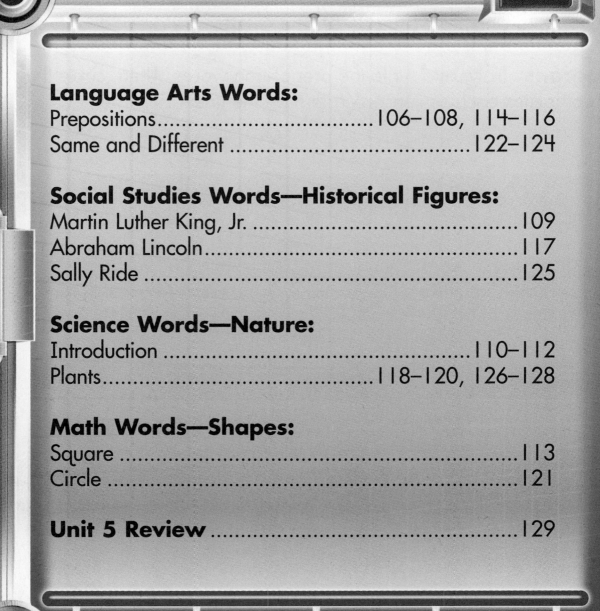

Name:_____

Words That Are Prepositions

Prepositions are words that show a connection between a noun or pronoun and another word. **Over** and **under** are prepositions.

Directions: Trace and write the preposition words. Then, circle the word that completes each sentence. Write it on the line.

over over _____

under under _____

1. The kite is _____ the tree.
over   under

2. The kite is _____ the tree.
over   under

UNIT 5

Name:_____

Words That Are Prepositions

Prepositions are words that show a connection between a noun or pronoun and another word. **Above** and **below** are prepositions.

Directions: Trace and write the preposition words. Then, circle the word that completes each sentence. Write it on the line.

above above -

below below -

1. The fish is _____ the water.
        above   below

2. The fish is _____ the water.
        above   below

Name:_____

Words That Are Prepositions

A **preposition** is a word that shows a connection between a noun or pronoun and another word. **Inside** and **outside** are prepositions.

Directions: Trace and write the preposition words. Then, circle the word that completes each sentence. Write it on the line.

UNIT 5

inside inside -

outside outside -

1. The dog is _____ his house.

        inside   outside

2. The dog is _____ his house.

        inside   outside

Name:_____

Words About Historical Figures

Martin Luther King, Jr. was an important black leader of the civil rights movement. Martin Luther King Day is a holiday we celebrate in January to honor his birthday.

Directions: Trace the words.

Martin Luther King, Jr.

civil rights

holiday

Directions: Martin Luther King, Jr.'s birthday is January 15. The holiday we use to honor him is celebrated each year on the third Monday of January. On the calendar below, color Martin Luther King, Jr.'s birthday red. Then, color the day it is celebrated blue.

January

SUN	MON	TUE	WED	THU	FRI	SAT
		1	2	3	4	5
6	7	8	9	10	11	12
13	14	15	16	17	18	19
20	21	22	23	24	25	26
27	28	29	30	31		

African-American Patriots

109

© 2007 School Specialty Publishing

Name:_____

Words About Nature

Directions: Trace and write the nature words. The first one is done for you.

   tree   tree

   grass

   flower

   pond

   sand

   sky

Name:_____

Words About Nature

Directions: Write the missing letter or letters for each word. The first one is done for you.

tree   tree

gr_ss   __ a __

fl__er   __ __ ow __

p_nd   __ o __

s_nd   __ a __

sk_   __ __ y

UNIT 5

Name:_____

Words About Nature

Directions: The letters in each word are mixed up. Unscramble the letters and write each word correctly.

etre

srags

loefwr

dnop

dnsa

yks

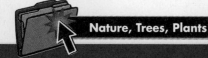

Nature, Trees, Plants

Name:_____

Shape Words

A **square** is a figure with four corners and four sides of the same length. This is a square:

Directions: Circle the squares. Then, trace and write the word. Color the picture.

square ---------------------------

UNIT 5

Name:_____

Words That Are Prepositions

A **preposition** is a word that shows a connection between a noun or pronoun and another word. **Up** and **down** are prepositions.

Directions: Trace and write the preposition words. Then, circle the word that completes each sentence. Write it on the line.

up ## up

down ## down

1. The flag is _____ the pole.

up   down

2. The flag is _____ the pole.

up   down

UNIT 5

Name:_____

Words That Are Prepositions

Directions: Look at each picture. Circle the correct preposition for each sentence. Write it on the line. Then, color the pictures.

Molly puts _____ the umbrella.

     up   on   in

The tie is _____ the bed.

     up   on   in

The cat is _____ the house.

     up   on   in

The bird flies _____ .

     up   on   in

He puts _____ mittens.

     up   on   in

The dog is _____ the rain.

     up   on   in

UNIT 5

Name:_____

Words That Are Prepositions

Directions: Read each sentence. Draw the sheep where it belongs. Then, color the pictures.

The sheep is on the table.	The sheep is under the loom.
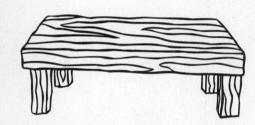	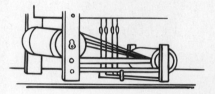 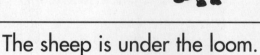
The sheep is in the berry bush.	The sheep is beside the cloth.
	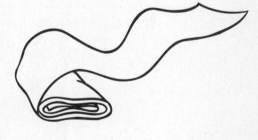
The sheep is on Charlie's hat.	The sheep is between the pieces of Charlie's cloak.
	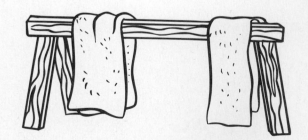

UNIT 5

Name:_____

Words About Historical Figures

Abraham Lincoln was born in a log cabin. He became the 16th president of the United States of America. He is known for his top hat and his beard.

Directions: Use the words in the Word Bank to fill in the lines next to each picture. Then, color the pictures.

Word Bank		
log cabin	top hat	ax
White House	book	beard

Abraham Lincoln as a boy

Abraham Lincoln as president

UNIT 5

Name: _____

Words About Plants

Directions: Use the words in the Word Bank to label each plant part. Read about the job of each plant part. Then, follow the directions to color the plant.

UNIT 5

Word Bank	
roots	stem
flower	leaf

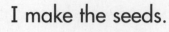

I make the seeds.

- - - - - - - - - - - - - - - - - - -

I make food for the plant.

- - - - - - - - - - - - - - - - - - -

I take water from the roots to the leaves.

- - - - - - - - - - - - - - - - - - -

I hold the plant in the ground.

- - - - - - - - - - - - - - - - - - -

Color the roots red.
Color the stem yellow.
Color the leaves green.
Color the flower your
  favorite color.

Name:_____

Words About Flowers

Directions: Read about flowers. Then, write the answers.

Some flowers grow in pots. Many flowers grow in flower beds. Others grow beside the road. Flowers begin as seeds. They grow into small buds. Then, they open wide and bloom. Flowers are pretty!

1. Name two places flowers grow.

_____

_____

2. Flowers begin as _____.

3. Flowers grow into small _____.

4. Then, flowers open wide and _____.

UNIT 5

Name:_____

Words About Flowers

Directions: Use the words in the Word Bank to complete the puzzle about flowers.

Across
2. Flowers do this when they open wide.
3. Flowers grow from these.

Down
1. A flower can grow in a flower bed or a ___.
2. Before they bloom, flowers grow___.

UNIT 5

 Plants

120

Name:_____

Shape Words

A **circle** is a figure that is round. This is a circle:

Directions: Draw squares around the circles. Then, trace and write the word. Color the picture.

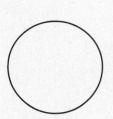
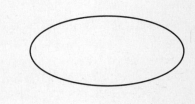

circle

Name:_____

Words for Similarities and Differences

Reading to find out how things are **alike** or **different** can help you picture and remember what you read. Things that are alike are called **similarities**. Things that are not alike are called **differences**.

> **Similarity:** Beth and Michelle are both girls.
> **Difference:** Beth has short hair, but Michelle has long hair.

Directions: Read the story. Then, color the dresses to show how they are alike and different.

Michelle and Beth are wearing new dresses. Both dresses are striped and have four buttons. Each dress has a belt and a pocket. Beth's dress is blue and white, while Michelle's is yellow and white. The stripes on Beth's dress go up and down. Stripes on Michelle's dress go from side to side. Beth's pocket is bigger with room for a kitten.

Beth's Dress

Michelle's Dress

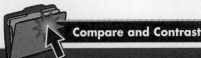
UNIT 5

Name:_____

Words for Similarities and Differences

Directions: The pages of your cut-and-fold book are on the back of this page. First, follow the directions below to make the book. Then, read your book to a family member or friend. Think of other things that are alike and different.

1. Tear the page out of the book.

2. Fold page along Line A so that the top meets the bottom. Make sure Line A is on the outside of the fold.

LINE A

3. Fold along Line B to make the book.

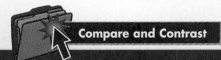
UNIT 5

UNIT 5

3

He is sad.

He is happy.

Line A

Line B

2

She is short.

She is tall.

The elephant is big.

The mouse is little.

4

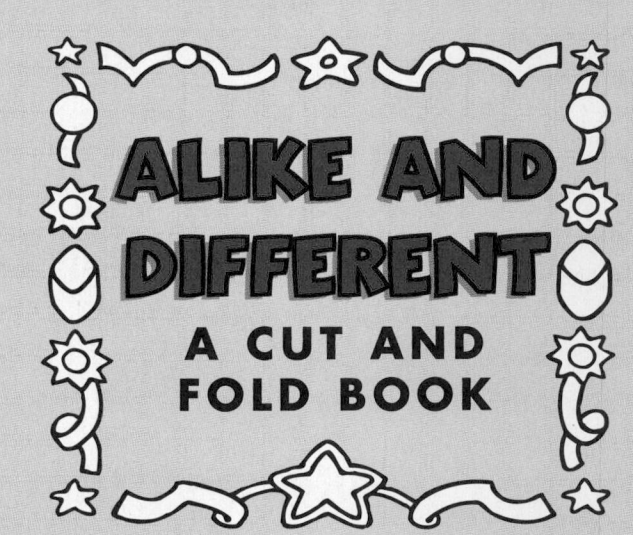

ALIKE AND DIFFERENT
A CUT AND FOLD BOOK

1

Name:_____

Words About Historical Figures

Sally Ride was the first American woman in space.

Directions: Trace and write the words. Then, color the picture.

Sally Ride

woman

space

First woman
in space—
June 1983

UNIT 5

Name:_____

Words About Plants

Directions: Use the words in the Word Bank to write the correct plant word under each picture.

Word Bank				
pumpkin	seed	sprout	flower	plant

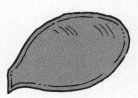

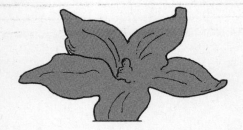

Name:_____

Words About Seeds

Seeds travel from one place to another. Sometimes people move the seeds. Sometimes they are moved in other ways.

Directions: Use the words in the word bank to finish the sentences to tell how seeds travel.

Word Bank

people

animals

animals

wind

water

Seeds travel with _____ .

Seeds travel in _____ .

Seeds travel on _____ .

Seeds travel with _____ .

Seeds travel on the _____ .

UNIT 5

Name:_____

Words About Seeds

Plants have seeds. Some plants have one seed. Other plants have many seeds. When the seeds are planted, they grow into new plants.

Directions: Use the words in the Word Bank to write the correct plant name under each picture. Count the seeds. Write the number of seeds beside the box. Then, draw a line from each seed to the correct plant.

Word Bank
pine
corn
peach
bean

_____ seeds

_____ seeds

_____ seed

_____ seeds

UNIT 5

Name:_____

Unit 5 Review

Directions: Circle the preposition word in each row.

1.	tree	above	beard
2.	leaf	space	inside
3.	under	grass	wind
4.	different	seeds	down
5.	square	on	sky
6.	in	roots	people

Directions: Write a sentence to tell how Abraham Lincoln and Martin Luther King, Jr. are similar. Then, write a sentence to tell how they are different.

- -

- -

- -

129

UNIT 5

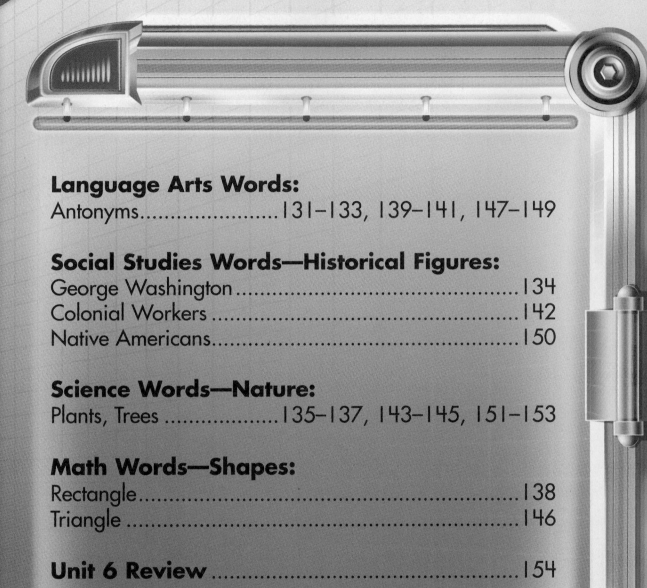

UNIT 6

Name:_____

Words That Are Opposites

Opposites are things that are different in every way.

Directions: Draw a line from each word to its opposite.

day

happy

big

open

front

little

closed

night

back

sad

Name:_____

Words That Are Opposites

Directions: Read each sentence and look at the first picture in each row. Then, look at the next picture. Use a word in the Word Bank to write a sentence that tells about it. The first one is done for you.

Word Bank			
found	new	big	last

 1. The dog is little.

 ## The dog is big.

 2. His book is lost.

_____

_ _

 3. The dog eats first.

_ _

_____

 4. I like my old shirt.

_ _

UNIT 6

Name:_____

Words That Are Opposites

Directions: Find the object in the picture that shows the opposite of each word. Write the object on the line.

1. low _____

2. cold _____

3. dry _____

4. short _____

5. noisy _____

6. hard _____

UNIT 6

Name:_____

Words About Historical Figures

George Washington was the first president of the United States of America. He appears on the dollar bill.

Directions: Connect the dots, beginning with number 1.
Color the dollar bill.
Then write: George Washington was our first president.

Name: _____

Words About Trees

Directions: Use the words in the Word Bank to complete the puzzle about trees.

Word Bank
- roots
- seeds
- trunk
- sun
- green

Across

1. Plants and trees need light from the _____ to grow.

2. The _____ hold plants and trees in the ground.

4. Leaves must be _____ to make food for plants and trees.

Down

1. Little _____ grow up to be plants and trees.

3. Most of the tree is held above the ground by the _____ .

Name:_____

Words About Leaves

Leaves make food for trees. Leaves use sunlight to make food. In the fall, they drop to the ground. You can find many shapes and colors of leaves.

Directions: Go outside. Compare the leaves you find with the leaves below. Circle the leaves that look like those you find. Color the leaves on this page.

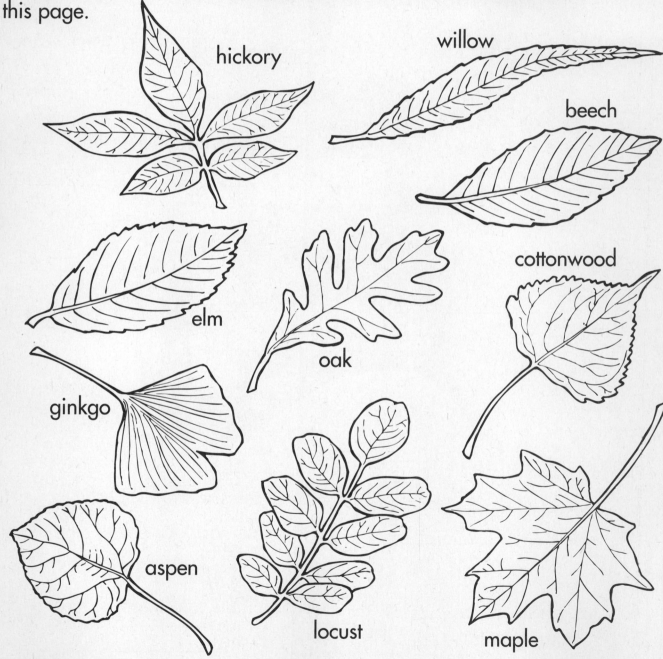

hickory

willow

beech

elm

oak

cottonwood

ginkgo

aspen

locust

maple

Name: _____

Words About Leaves

Leaves are like little factories. They make food for the tree. Leaves need sunshine, air, and water to make food.

Leaves change in the fall. They lose their green color. Then, they cannot make food for the tree.

Directions: On the left side of the box, draw a leaf that can make food. Color it green.
On the right side of the box, draw a leaf that cannot make food. Color it red.
Circle the correct word for each sentence. Write it on the line.

| | |
| | |

1. Food is made by _____ leaves.

     green   yellow

2. Leaves need _____ to make food.

     shade   sunshine

3. Leaves _____ make food in the fall.

     can   cannot

Name:_____

Shape Words

A **rectangle** is a figure with four corners and four sides. The sides opposite each other are the same length.
This is a rectangle:

Directions: Circle each rectangle. Then, trace and write the word.

rectangle ---------------------------

Name:_____

Words That Are Opposites

Directions: Color the spaces yellow if they have word pairs with opposite meanings.
Color the spaces blue if they have word pairs with similar meanings.

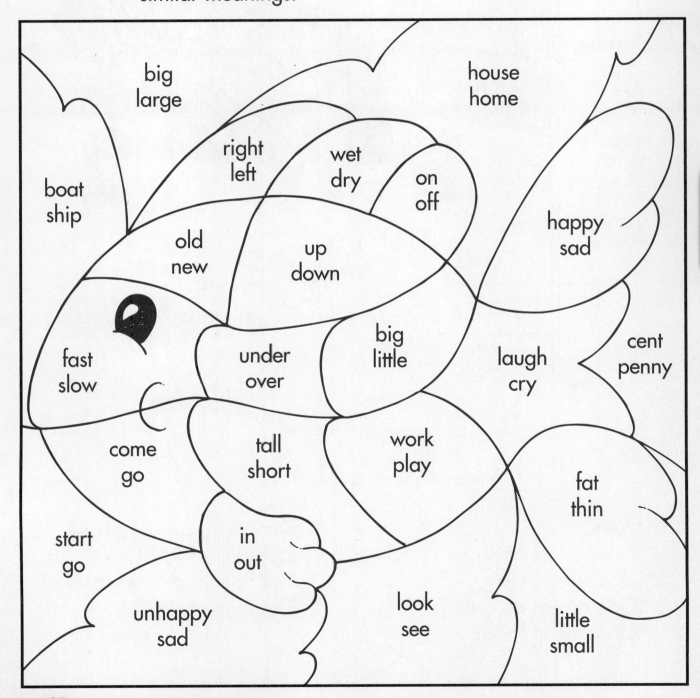

UNIT 6

Name: _____

Words That Are Opposites

Directions: Use the words in the Word Bank to complete the puzzle about opposites.

Word Bank

high   yes   left

heavy   tight

safe   full

Across
1. Opposite of **low**
2. Opposite of **no**
4. Opposite of **empty**
6. Opposite of **loose**

Down
1. Opposite of **light**
3. Opposite of **dangerous**
5. Opposite of **right**

Name:_____

Words That Are Opposites

Some words are opposites. **Opposites** are things that are different in every way. **Dark** and **light** are opposites.

Directions: Trace and write the words. The first one is done for you.

new   new

old

big

little

lost

found

Antonyms

141

© 2007 School Specialty Publishing

Name:_____

Words About Historical Figures

The first thirteen states to make up the United States began as **colonies**.
Colonists were the people who lived in or were members of the colonies.
They had many different jobs.

Directions: Draw shoes in the window for the shoemaker.
Draw dough for the baker to make bread.
Draw a hammer in the blacksmith's hand.
Draw a dress on the hanger for the dressmaker.
Draw a saddle for the saddlemaker.
Draw sacks of flour and sugar for the storekeeper.

Blacksmith

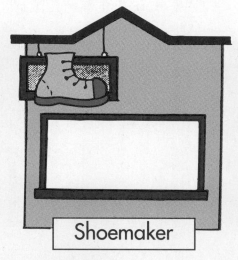

Storekeeper

Dressmaker

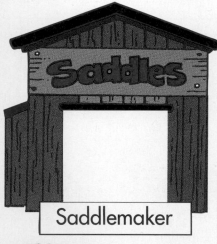

Saddlemaker

Shoemaker

Baker

UNIT 6

Name:_____

Words About Trees

Trees have three main parts: the trunk, the roots, and the leaves. Each part has a special job.

Directions: Cut out the name of each tree part. Cut out the job of each part. Glue them onto the picture in their correct places.

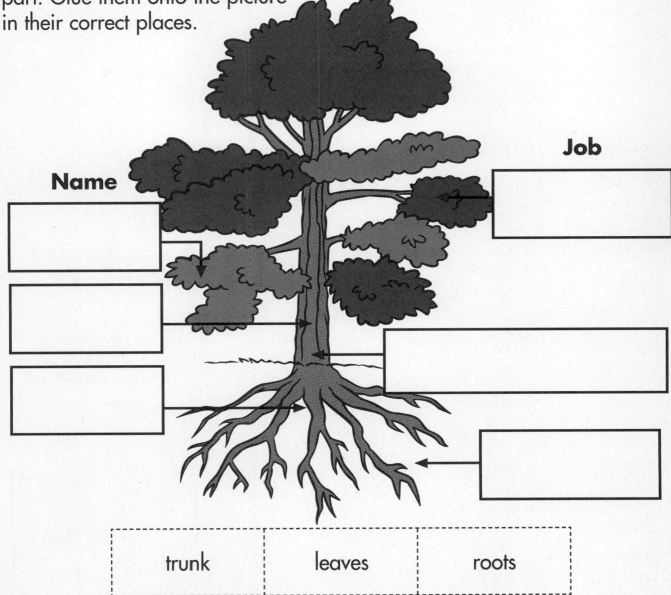

Name

Job

trunk	leaves	roots

| I hold the tree in the ground. | I make food for the tree. | I hold most of the tree above the ground. |

UNIT 6

Page left blank for cutting activity.

Name:_____

Words About Trees

Some trees drop their seeds in the spring. Other trees drop their seeds in the fall. The seeds grow up. Do you know what they grow up to be?

Directions: Write **first**, **second**, or **third** under each picture to show how the acorn grows into a mighty oak tree. Color the pictures. Then, complete the sentence below.

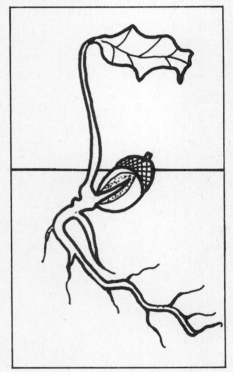
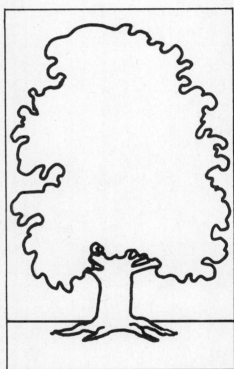
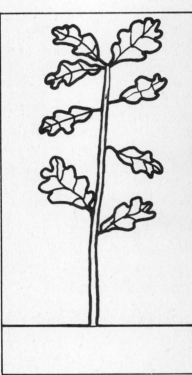

UNIT 6

- - - - - - - - - - - - - - - - - -   - - - - - - - - - - - - - - - - -   - - - - - - - - - - - - - - -

I am a little acorn. One day, _____

- -

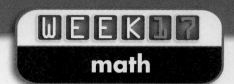

Name:_____

Shape Words

A **triangle** is a figure with three corners and three sides.
This is a triangle:

Directions: Circle each triangle. Then, trace and write the word.

triangle -

UNIT 6

Name:_____

Words That Are Antonyms

Words with opposite meanings are called **antonyms**.

Directions: Circle the correct antonym for each underlined word.

1. The sky was very <u>dark</u>.   purple   old   light

2. Turn <u>left</u> at the light.   right   sideways   yellow

3. The shelf was very <u>high</u>.   pretty   low   loud

4. The turtle walked <u>slowly</u>.   silly   quickly   nicely

5. I <u>whispered</u> at the circus.   laughed   coughed   shouted

6. Bobby is an <u>adult</u>.   child   fan   principal

7. The clown was very <u>strong</u>.   weak   silly   hungry

8. The library is a <u>quiet</u> place.   fun   messy   noisy

Words That Are Antonyms

Antonyms are words that have opposite meanings. **Old** and **new** are antonyms. **Laugh** and **cry** are antonyms, too.

Directions: Use the words in the Word Bank to write the correct antonym under each picture.

Word Bank

down

go

left

sad

dry

stop

----

happy

----

right

----

up

----

wet

Antonyms

148

UNIT 6

Name:_____

Words That Are Antonyms

Directions: Look at each picture. Then, write the answer to the question.

Example: Is the cookie big?

No, the cookie is little.

1. Has the boy found his boat?

_____
- -
_____

2. Will he go first?

_____
- -
_____

3. Is the sky dark?

_____
- -
_____

Antonyms

UNIT 6

Name:_____

Words About Historical Figures

Native Americans lived in tribes in North America, South America, and Central America before the people of Europe began to settle.

Directions: Write **tepee** in box 1.
Write **adobe** in box 2.
Write **wigwam** in box 3.
Write **longhouse** in box 4.
Draw a sun on the teepee.
Color the longhouse brown.
Draw small windows on the adobe.

1.

2.

3.

4.

Name:_____

Words About Trees

People eat many foods from trees. Animals can also eat the food from trees. The food comes from different parts of the tree.

Directions: Draw an **X** on the foods that do not come from trees. Use the words in the Word Bank to label each food that people can get from trees.

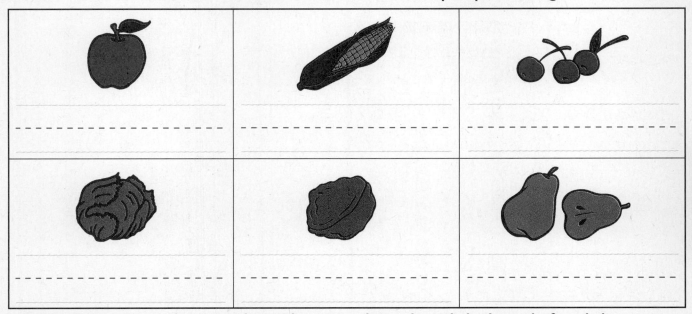

Directions: Use the words in the Word Bank to label each food that animals can get from trees.

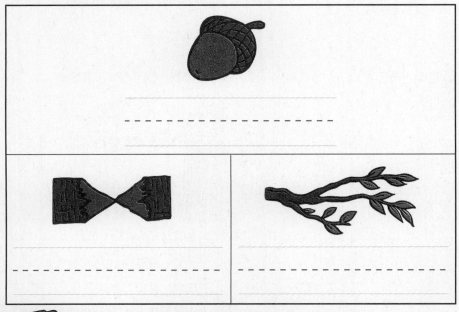

Word Bank

acorn

nut

leaves

apple

bark

cherries

pear

UNIT 6

Name:_____

Words About Trees

There are many kinds of trees. Each kind has a different name.

Directions: Use the words in the Word Bank to find the tree names. Look sideways.

```
O A K
A P P L E
P E C A N U L G H T
X Y O X S P R U C E
W A L N U T Z O M T
H B R W O R A N G E
C H E R R Y L E R X
B T R O L X P I N E
C E D A R H M T E R
```

Word Bank
oak
apple
cherry
pine
walnut
cedar
spruce
orange
pecan

Some of the trees above are fruit trees. Some are nut trees. Some are evergreen trees.

Directions: Use the words in the Word Bank to write the correct tree names in each list.

Fruit	**Nut**	**Evergreen**
_____	_____	_____
_____	_____	_____
_____	_____	_____

UNIT 6

Words About Plants

We eat many plant parts. Sometimes, we eat just the fruit. Sometimes, we eat just the leaves. We also might eat the stem, the root, or the seeds.

Directions: Draw a line from each plant part to its name. Then, color the plant parts. The first one is done for you.

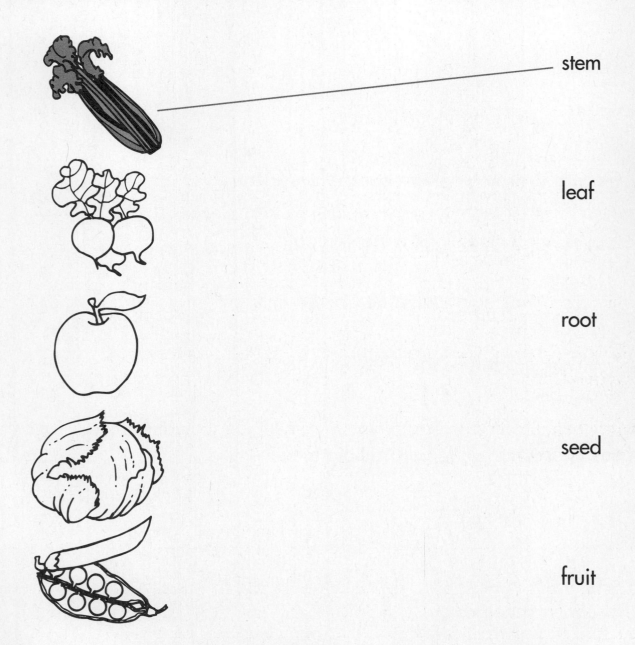

stem

leaf

root

seed

fruit

UNIT 6

Name:_____

Unit 6 Review

Directions: Read each sentence. The underlined word makes the sentence wrong. Write the opposite of the word to correct each sentence.

1. I was <u>happy</u> when I lost my dog.

2. It is <u>hot</u> in the winter.

3. You must be <u>noisy</u> in the library.

4. George Washington was our <u>last</u> president.

5. Leaves need <u>moonlight</u> to make food.

6. His glass was <u>empty</u> after he poured milk in it.

7. It is <u>dangerous</u> to wear a helmet when you ride a bike.

8. Seeds grow <u>down</u> to become big trees.

9. A turtle walks <u>quickly</u>.

10. Leaves <u>can</u> make food for the tree when they lose their green color.

UNIT 6

Words That Are Synonyms

Synonyms are words that have almost the same meaning. **Tired** and **sleepy** are synonyms. **Talk** and **speak** are synonyms.

Directions: Read each word. Use the words on the anthill to write the correct synonym on each line.

1. glad _____

2. little _____

3. begin _____

4. above _____

5. damp _____

6. large _____

wet

big

happy

over

small

start

UNIT 7

Synonyms

156

© 2007 School Specialty Publishing

Words That Are Synonyms

Directions: Circle the word in each row that is most like the first word in the row. The first one is done for you.

1. grin   (smile) frown mad

2. bag   jar sack box

3. cat   fruit animal flower

4. apple  rot cookie fruit

5. brown  tan black red

6. bird  dog cat duck

UNIT 7

Name:_____

Words That Are Synonyms

Directions: Read the story. Use the words in the Word Bank to write the correct synonym on each line.

Word Bank
market
ran   fruit
coins   fast

Dan went to the _____.
store

He wanted to buy _____.
food

He walked very _____.
quickly

The store had what he wanted.

He bought it using _____.
dimes

Instead of walking, Dan _____.
jogged

UNIT 7

Name:_____

Holiday Words

The pilgrims celebrated their first harvest with the Native Americans who had helped them. This celebration became known as **Thanksgiving**.

Directions: Use the words in the Word Bank to find the hidden foods. Then, color the picture.

corn	pumpkin	squash	turkey
onion	beans	berries	fish

UNIT 7

Name:_____

Food Words

Directions: Trace and write the food words. Then, color the pictures. The first one is done for you.

 bread   **bread**

 cookie

 apple

 cake

 milk

 egg

 Food   160   © 2007 School Specialty Publishing

Name:_____

Food Words

Directions: Complete each sentence with the correct food word. Use the pictures to help you.

Kim got up in the morning.

"Do you want an _____  ?" her mother asked.

"Yes, please," Kim said.

"May I have some _____ , too?"

"Okay," her mother said.

"How about some _____ ?" Kim asked.

Her mother laughed. "Not now," she said.

She put an _____ in Kim's lunch.

"Do you want a _____ or some

_____ today?"

"Both!" Kim said.

UNIT 7

Name:_____

Food Words

Directions: Use the words in the Word Bank to complete the puzzle about food.

Across
3. It comes from cows.
5. It can go in a pie.
7. It is good with jelly.

Down
1. It is brown and sweet.
2. Rabbits like them.
4. It is made from milk.
6. It can be red, yellow, or green.
8. It is yellow and grows in a bunch.

Word Bank			
apple	peanut butter	cheese	carrots
cherry	raisin	milk	banana

UNIT 7

Name:_____

Shape Words

An **oval** is an egg-shaped figure. This is an oval: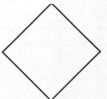

A **diamond** is a figure with four sides of the same length. Its corners form points at the top, sides, and bottom. This is a diamond:

Directions: Color the ovals red. Color the diamonds blue. Then, trace and write the words.

 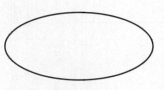 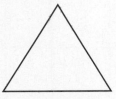 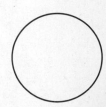

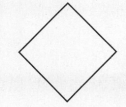 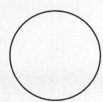 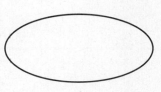 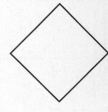

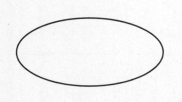  

oval

diamond

UNIT 7

Name:_____

Words That Are Synonyms

Synonyms are words that mean almost the same thing. **Start** and **begin** are synonyms.

Directions: Look at each picture. Use the words in the Word Bank to write the correct synonyms in each box.

small	funny	large	sad	silly	little	big	unhappy

Name:_____

Words That Are Synonyms

Directions: Look at each picture. Use the words in the Word Bank to write the correct synonyms in each box.

Word Bank
rocks   start   road   begin   street   stones   sad   unhappy

UNIT 7

Name:_____

Words That Are Synonyms

Directions: Circle the synonym in each square that has the same meaning or close to the same meaning as the word in bold print. The first one is done for you.

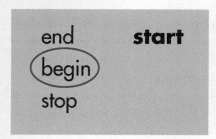

end **start**	scream **shout**	cat **sick**
(begin)	brother	bath
stop	talk	ill

Directions: Think of a synonym for each of the three words listed. Then, write a sentence using both words.

1. smart/_____

_____

_____

2. bad/_____

_____

_____

3. little/_____

_____

_____

UNIT 7

Name:_____

Holiday Words

Holidays begin with capital letters.

Directions: Use the words in the Word Bank to write the correct holiday name under each picture.

Word Bank	
Fourth of July	Valentine's Day
Presidents' Day	Thanksgiving

_____

- -

_____

- -

UNIT 7

Name:_____

Food Words

Fruit comes from plants. It is sweet.

Directions: Look at each picture and food word. Then, write the names of the fruits on the lines.

apple

banana

grapes

potato

orange

carrot

broccoli

_____   _____

_ _ _ _ _ _ _ _ _ _ _ _ _ _ _ _   _ _ _ _ _ _ _ _ _ _ _ _ _ _ _ _

_____   _____

_ _ _ _ _ _ _ _ _ _ _ _ _ _ _ _   _ _ _ _ _ _ _ _ _ _ _ _ _ _ _ _

Name:_____

Food Words

Vegetables grow in gardens. Vegetables help to keep people healthy.

Directions: Look at each picture and food word. Then, write the names of the vegetables on the lines. Think of one more vegetable to add on the last line.

bread   beans

lettuce   banana

noodles   carrot

broccoli   peas

UNIT 7

Drink Words

Directions: Circle the pictures of things you can drink. Then, write the names of those things on the lines.

milk

ice

soup and crackers

juice

soda

ice-cream bar

- -

-        -

Name:_____

Shape Words

Directions: Use the words in the Word Bank to find the shape words. Look up, down, and sideways. Then, color the shapes.

```
r  p  m  s  q  u  a  r  e  a
w  e  n  h  e  o  f  e  t  g
d  i  a  m  o  n  d  c  d  o
a  k  u  l  n  y  i  t  b  v
p  v  y  s  d  r  c  a  j  a
c  i  r  c  l  e  n  n  c  l
f  t  z  w  o  v  z  g  l  u
k  q  x  x  i  b  m  l  g  h
t  r  i  a  n  g  l  e  s  j
```

Word Bank

square	rectangle	oval
diamond	circle	triangle

  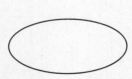

UNIT 7

Name:_____

Words That Are Synonyms

Directions: Read each sentence. Use the words in the Word Bank to write the correct synonym for each underlined word. The first one is done for you.

Word Bank	
pick	tired
porch	pull

1. I was so <u>sleepy</u> I couldn't wait to go

to bed! tired

2. Please <u>choose</u> a present you would like

to open.

3. Are you strong enough to <u>drag</u> this

heavy crate?

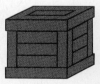

4. We sipped lemonade on the <u>deck</u>.

UNIT 7

Name:_____

Words That Are Synonyms

Directions: Read each sentence. Circle the correct synonym for each underlined word. Then, write the new words on the lines.

1. The boy was <u>mad</u>.   happy   angry   pup

2. The <u>dog</u> is brown.   pup   cat   rat

3. I like to <u>scream</u>.   soar   mad   shout

4. The bird can <u>fly</u>.   soar   jog   warm

5. The girl can <u>run</u>.   sleep   jog   shout

6. I am <u>hot</u>.   warm   cold   soar

- - - - - - - - - - - - - - - - - - -   - - - - - - - - - - - - - - - - - - -   - - - - - - - - - - - - - - - - - - -

- - - - - - - - - - - - - - - - - - -   - - - - - - - - - - - - - - - - - - -   - - - - - - - - - - - - - - - - - - -

Synonyms   **173**

UNIT 7

Name:_____

Words That Are Synonyms

Directions: Use the words in the Word Bank to write the correct synonym on each line.

Word Bank			
bright	hop	dad	fast
pretty	plate	silly	center

 sunny _____

_____

 beautiful _____

_____

 middle _____

_____

 dish _____

_____

 quick _____

_____

 jump _____

_____

 goofy _____

_____

 father _____

_____

 Synonyms

174

© 2007 School Specialty Publishing

UNIT 7

Name:_____

Words About Voting

To **vote** is to express a choice in a decision. In the United States of America, people vote on many different things. People decide on the president by voting.

Directions: Senators represent people from different areas of the country. They vote on many issues. Write a letter to your state senator about a problem you would like him or her to solve.

- -

(date)

- -

(address)

- -

Dear Senator - - - - - - - - - - - - - - - - ,

- -

- -

- -

Sincerely,

- - - - - - - - - - - - - - - - - - -

UNIT 7

Name:_____

Food Words

Directions: Draw a meal you like to eat. Draw one meat, one fruit or vegetable, one bread, and one dairy food. Then, answer the questions.

_____

- -

1. What is your meat? _____

_____

- -

2. What is your fruit or vegetable? _____

_____

- -

3. What is your bread? _____

_____

- -

4. What is your dairy food? _____

Name:_____

Food Words

Directions: Use the words in the Word Bank to write the correct food in each food group.

Word Bank

ham   bagel   pear
bean   pie   yogurt

VEGETABLE

GRAIN

FRUIT

DAIRY

SWEET

MEAT

UNIT 7

Name:_____

Food Words

Directions: Use the words in the Word Bank to write the correct food names in each food group.

Word Bank

carrots	cherries	chicken	cheese	fish	ham
cake	lettuce	bagel	oranges	pears	rolls
beans	toast	pie	yogurt		
cottage cheese		candy bar			

Dairy

Meats

Fruits

Sweets

Vegetables

Grains

UNIT 7

Name:_____

Unit 7 Review

Directions: Draw a line from each word to its synonym.

start	jog
dish	little
small	begin
run	tired
sleepy	plate

Directions: The letters in each word are mixed up. Unscramble the letters and write each word correctly.

1. catorr

_____

2. daber

_____

3. epalp

_____

4. ipe

_____

5. heseec

_____

Directions: Write the holiday word correctly.

_____

thanksgiving

UNIT 8

Name:_____

Compound Words

Some short words can be put together to make one new word. The new word is called a **compound word**.

Example: cow + boy = cowboy

Directions: Look at each pair of pictures and words. Join together the two words to make a compound word. Write it on the line.

rain + coat =

_____

door + bell =

_____

dog + house =

_____

pan + cake =

_____

horse + shoe =

_____

© 2007 School Specialty Publishing

UNIT 6

Compound Words

Directions: Write the two words that make up each compound word.

1. snowball   --------------- ---------------

2. raincoat  --------------- ---------------

3. airplane   --------------- ---------------

4. watermelon   --------------- ---------------

5. haircut  --------------- ---------------

6. football   --------------- ---------------

7. sunshine   --------------- ---------------

UNIT 8

Name:_____

Compound Words

Directions: Underline the two words in each sentence that can make a compound word. Write the compound word on the line to complete the sentence.

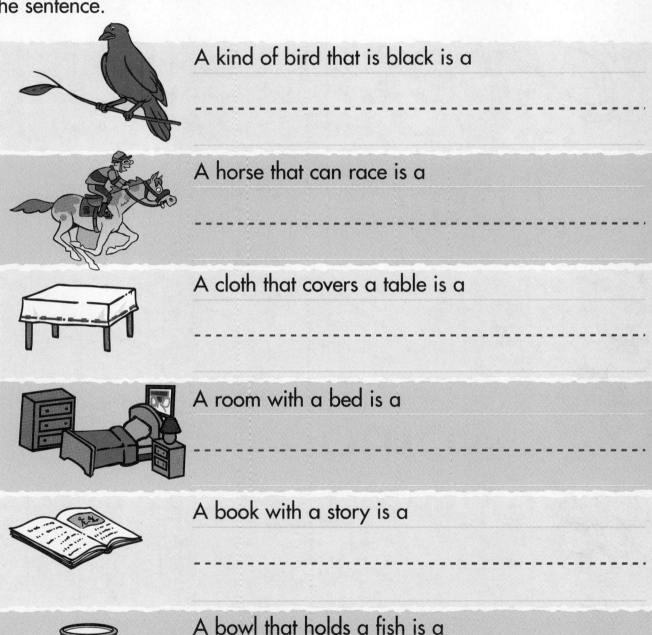

A kind of bird that is black is a

_____ .

A horse that can race is a

_____ .

A cloth that covers a table is a

_____ .

A room with a bed is a

_____ .

A book with a story is a

_____ .

A bowl that holds a fish is a

_____ .

UNIT 8

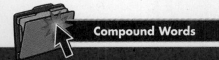

Name:_____

People Words

Directions: Trace and write the people words.

 girl

 boy

 man

 woman

 people

 children

UNIT 8

Name:_____

Words About the Human Body

Directions: Trace and write the human body words.

head --------------------------------

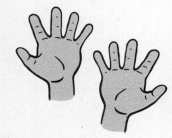
hands --------------------------------

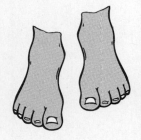
feet --------------------------------

legs --------------------------------

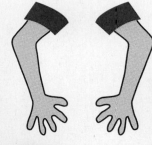
arms --------------------------------

UNIT 8

Human Body

185

Name:_____

Words About the Human Body

Directions: The letters in each word are mixed up. Unscramble the letters and write each word correctly.

Example:  adhe head

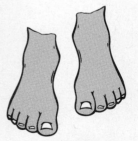 sdnah

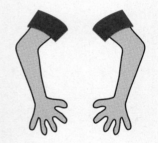 smra

 eetf

  slge

UNIT 8

Name:_____

Words About the Human Body

Directions: Use the words in the Word Bank to complete each sentence with the correct human body part. Put a period at the end of each telling sentence and a question mark at the end of each asking sentence.

Example:  I wear my hat on my

Word Bank			
arms	legs	feet	hands

1. How strong are your _____ ☐

2. You wear shoes on your _____ ☐

3. If you're happy and you know it, clap your _____ ☐

4. My pants cover my _____ ☐

Human Body

187

UNIT 8

Name:_____

Time Words

Directions: Use the words in the Word Bank and the clock to complete each sentence with the correct time word.

Word Bank		
circle	hands	twelve
face	six	clock

This machine works all day and night.
We never turn it off.

It has a _____ (A),
but no eyes and no nose!

It has _____ (B, C), but no fingers.

The little hand (B) is pointing to _____ .

The big hand (C) is pointing to _____ .

This machine is shaped like a _____ . (D)

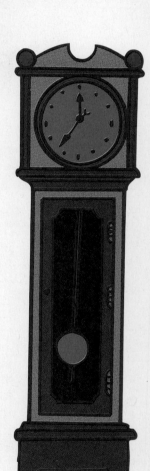

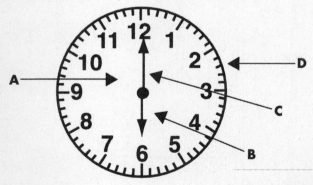

This machine is called a _____ .

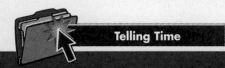

Name:_____

Compound Words

Directions: Cut out the pictures and words at the bottom of the page. Glue two words together to make a compound word. Write it on the line.

☐ + ☐ = -

☐ + ☐ = -

☐ + ☐ = -

☐ + ☐ = -

cut -

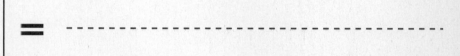			
mail	snow	ball	bow
basket	man	rain	box

UNIT 8

Page left blank for cutting activity.

UNIT 8

Name:_____

Compound Words

Directions: Draw lines to make compound words. Write the new words on the lines.

Example: song + bird = songbird

dog	room
foot	box
bed	house
mail	light
some	ball
moon	thing

UNIT 8

_ _ _ _ _ _ _ _ _ _ _ _ _ _ _ _ _ _ _ _

_ _ _ _ _ _ _ _ _ _ _ _ _ _ _ _ _ _ _ _

_ _ _ _ _ _ _ _ _ _ _ _ _ _ _ _ _ _ _ _

 **Compound Words**   **191**   © 2007 School Specialty Publishing

Name:_____

People Words

Directions: Complete each sentence with the correct people word. Use the pictures to help you.

_____
- -

1. The _____ was last in line at the toy store.

_____
- -

2. The _____ took a walk in the woods.

_____
- -

3. The _____ had to help her father.

_____
- -

4. The _____ had a surprise for the children.

_____
- -

5. Some _____ like to eat outside.

_____
- - - - - - - - - - - -

6. Something came out of the box when the _____ opened it.

UNIT 8

Name:_____

Words About the Human Body

Directions: Read the two sentences on each line. Draw a line between them. Then, write each sentence again. Begin each sentence with a capital letter. Put a period at the end of each telling sentence and a question mark at the end of each asking sentence.

Example: wash your hands I they are dirty

Wash your hands.
They are dirty.

1. you have big arms are you very strong

- -

- -

2. I have two feet I can run fast

- -

- -

UNIT 8

Name:_____

Words About the Human Body

Directions: Use the words in the Word Bank to answer each riddle.

Word Bank				
eyes	hair	mouth	nose	skin

1. There are two of me. We can blink. We can see. We can wink. We can weep.

   What are we? _____

2. There is one of me. I can sing. I can speak. I can eat. I can even blow a big bubble. I can eat ice cream, too.

   What am I? _____

3. There is one of me. If something tickles me, I will sneeze. I like to sniff flowers. I like the smell of hot dogs, also.

   What am I? _____

4. I can be almost any color. I can be long or short. I can be curled and I can be straight.

   What am I? _____

5. I cover a lot. I keep muscles, bones, and blood inside your body. I let you know if it is hot or cold outside. I tell you if something is wet or dry.

   What am I? _____

UNIT 8

Name:_____

Words About the Human Body

Directions: Use the words in the Word Bank to find the human body words. Look up, down, and sideways.

Word Bank

head	arm	foot	brain	skeleton
bone	skin	blood	heart	windpipe
lungs	eye	muscle	teeth	stomach

```
a t e e t h o y i u
n e s q h e a d r t
l u k w f a r u t s
l d e i o r m e s d
s k l n o t z y k e
o m e d t s b e i w
h e t p b r a i n i
t c o i q b l o o d
s a n p d o w b l s
w i m e p n i t u a
m u s c l e c l n e
s t o m a c h a g n
e r o y n k o r s h
```

Name:_____

Time Words

There are many ways to measure time. A **year** has 365 days in it. A **week** has 7 days in it. A **day** has 24 hours in it. An **hour** has 60 minutes in it. A **minute** has 60 seconds in it. A **second** goes very quickly.

Directions: Use the words in the Word Bank to complete the puzzle about time.

Word Bank				
day	year	minute	week	hour

5. ↓

1. ↓

3. →

4. →

2. →

1. ↓ 365 days make a y _____ .

2. → 7 days make a w _____ .

3. → 24 hours make a d _____ .

4. → 60 minutes make an h _____ .

5. ↓ 60 seconds make a m _____ .

UNIT 8

Name:_____

Compound Words

Directions: Cut out the cards below. Turn them over. Take turns with a partner trying to make compound words. When a player makes a compound word, he or she gets to keep the word.

Cut ✂ --

flash	snow	ball	sun
mail	house	plant	room
light	bow	light	card
base	shine	dog	box
rain	flake	thing	post
family	house	in	house
any	side	day	birth

Compound Words

UNIT 8

UNIT 8

Page left blank for cutting activity.

Name:_____

Compound Words

Directions: Use the words in the Word Bank to complete each sentence with the correct compound word.

Word Bank				
raincoat	bedroom	lunchbox	hallway	sandbox

1. A box with sand is a

   _____.

2. The way through a hall is a

   _____.

3. A box for lunch is a

   _____.

4. A coat for the rain is a

   _____.

5. A room with a bed is a

   _____.

UNIT 8

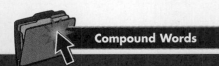
Compound Words   199   © 2007 School Specialty Publishing

Name:_____

People Words

Directions: Use the words in the Word Bank to find the people words. Look up, down, and sideways. One is done for you.

people	baby	boy	woman	girl	children	man
u	a	w		r	c	a
c	f	d	k		h	n
s	r	b	h		i	y
p	e	o		p	l	e
n	l	y		j	d	o
k	c	g		i	r	l
x	b	h	s		e	b
w	o	m		a	n	m
r	b	a		b	y	e
t	o	n		d	k	m

UNIT 8

Name:_____

Words About the Human Body

Bones give your body shape. They help you stand up tall. You cannot see your bones. But you can feel many of your bones under your skin.

Directions: Draw a line from each bone to the part of the body where it is found. Use the words in the Word Bank to label each bone.

Word Bank		
skull	ribs	foot
hand	knee	hips

UNIT 8

Name:_____

Words About the Human Body

Directions: Use the words in the Word Bank to complete the puzzle about the human body.

Across
3. They protect your heart and lungs.
6. All of your bones.
7. It connects your leg and foot.

Down
1. Found on the end of your hands.
2. Found on the end of your feet.
4. Your spine.
5. It makes your leg bend.
6. This protects your brain.

Word Bank
ribs   toes   fingers   knee
skull   backbone   ankle   skeleton

UNIT 8

Name:_____

Words About the Human Body

Directions: Use the words at the bottom of the page to complete the puzzle about the human body.

Across
2. You use these to breathe.
4. You need to do this when you're tired.
5. This breaks down food.
7. This tells your body what to do.
9. This is a gas you breathe.
10. It pumps blood.

Down
1. It carries oxygen to your body.
3. Tiny living things that can make you sick.
6. This helps you when you are sick.
8. These support and shape your body.

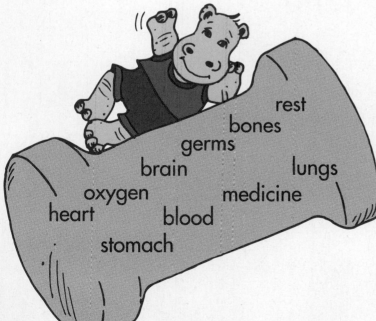

rest
bones
germs
brain   lungs
oxygen   medicine
heart   blood
stomach

UNIT 8

Name: _____

Unit 8 Review

Directions: Use a word in the Word Bank to write a complete sentence about your body.

Word Bank					
rib	arm	bone	muscle	knee	nose

_____

_____

Directions: Use the words in the Word Bank to write six compound words.

Word Bank					
pan	rain	ball	bed	coat	sun
cake	mail	foot	room	shine	box

1. _____   4. _____

2. _____   5. _____

3. _____   6. _____

Directions: Use the words in the Word Bank to write the time words in order from the least amount of time to the most.

Word Bank				
day	year	minute	week	hour

1. _____   4. _____

2. _____   5. _____

3. _____

UNIT 8

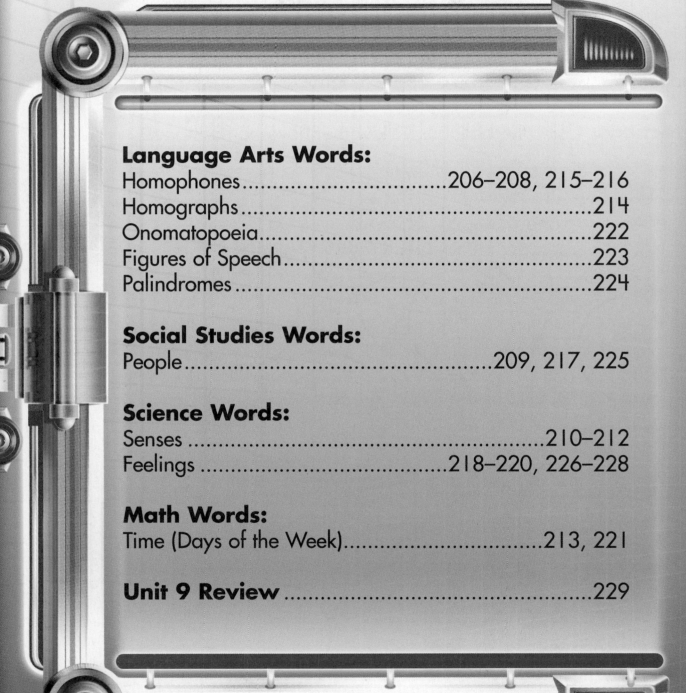

Name:_____

Words That Are Homophones

Homophones are words that sound the same but have different spellings and meanings. **Too** and **two** are homophones. So are **road** and **rode**.

Directions: Color the balloons yellow that have homophones.

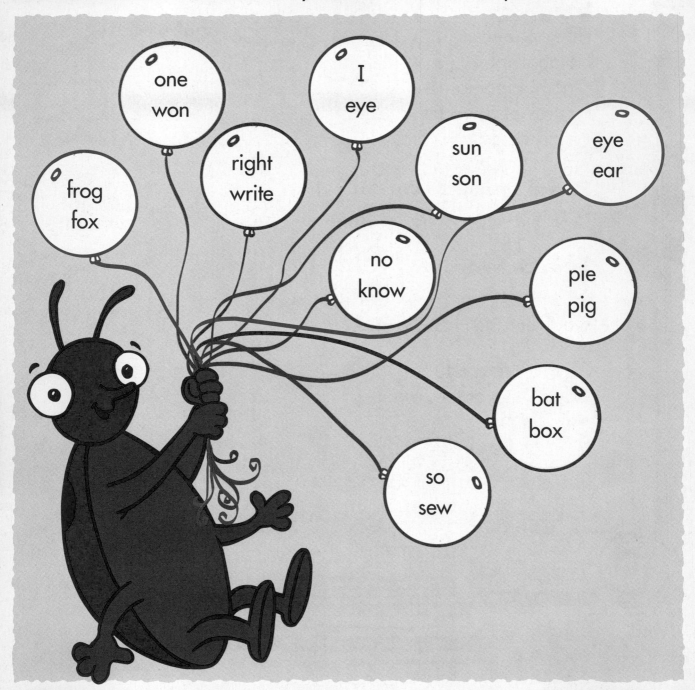

UNIT 9

Name: _____

Words That Are Homophones

Directions: Read each sentence. Underline the two words that sound the same but are spelled differently and mean something different.

1. Tom ate eight grapes.

2. Becky read *Little Red Riding Hood*.

3. I went to buy two dolls.

4. Five blue feathers blew in the wind.

5. Would you get wood for the fire?

UNIT 9

Name:_____

Words That Are Homophones

Directions: Complete each sentence with the correct homophone.

1. Jim _____ the cookies.

ate
eight

2. Sally has _____ pencils.

to
two

3. The _____ is bumpy.

rode
road

4. _____ can ride a bike.

Eye
I

5. Can you _____ the picture?

see
sea

6. Tom _____ up the balloon.

blew
blue

UNIT 9

Name:_____

People Words

Directions: Trace and write the people words. Then, circle the correct people word for each sentence. Write it on the line.

you and me you and me

1. I will play with _____ .   you   me

2. You can go with _____ .   you   me

3. Can you run with _____ ?   you   me

UNIT 9

Name:_____

Sense Words

Directions: Trace and write the sense words.

Example:

 taste taste

 touch

 smell

 see

 hear

UNIT 9

Name:_____

Sense Words

Directions: Circle the word in each row that is spelled correctly. Write it on the line.

Example:

tast
(taste)
tste

taste

touch
tuch
touh

_____

smel
smll
smell

_____

her
hear
har

_____

see
se
sea

_____

UNIT 9

Name:_____

Sense Words

Directions: Complete each sentence with the correct sense word. The first one is done for you.

taste
mouth I can **taste** things with my **mouth** .

touch
hands I can _____ things with my _____ .

nose
smell I can _____ things with my _____ .

hear
ears I can _____ things with my _____ .

see
eyes I can _____ things with my _____ .

UNIT 9

Senses

212

Name:_____

Time Words

The days of the week begin with capital letters.

Directions: Use the words in the Word Bank to write the days of the week in the correct order on the lines.

Tuesday

Saturday

Monday

Friday

Thursday

Sunday

Wednesday

Name: _____

Words That Are Homographs

Homographs are words that have more than one meaning.

Directions: Read each word and its meanings. Then, use the numbers to match each picture with the correct meaning.

cross: 1. to draw a line through
                2. angry

fall: 3. the season between summer and winter
                4. to trip or stumble

land: 5. to bring to a stop or rest
                6. the ground

_____   _____   _____

_____   _____   _____

Name:_____

Words That Are Homophones

Homophones are words that sound the same but are spelled differently and mean something different. **Blew** and **blue** are homophones.

Directions: Look at the word pairs. Circle the word that describes the picture. Write it on the line.

1. sew   so

_____

2. pair   pear

_____

3. eye   I

_____

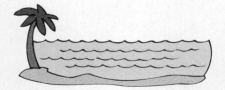

4. see   sea

_____

UNIT 9

Name: _____

Words That Are Homophones

Directions: Circle the word that matches the picture. Then, complete each sentence with the correct word.

1. This is a present _____ your birthday.

        four   for

2. Jane lost a _____ of new shoes.

        pair   pear

3. The boys will either swim _____ go to the ball game.

        oar   or

4. Let's _____ at eight o'clock.

        meet   meat

5. Old Mother Hubbard's cupboard was _____ .

        bear   bare

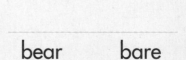

UNIT 9

 Homophones

216

Name:_____

People Words

Sometimes we use other words in place of people names. For **boy** or **man**, we can use the word **he**. For **girl** or **woman**, we can use the word **she**. For two or more people, we can use the word **they**.

Directions: Write **he**, **she**, or **they** to complete each sentence.

Example: The boy likes cars.

He _____ likes cars.

1. The girl is running fast.

_____ is running fast.

2. The man looks funny.

_____ looks funny.

3. The woman is a teacher.

_____ is a teacher.

4. The children like school.

_____ like school.

UNIT 9

Name:_____

Feeling Words

Directions: Use the words in the Word Bank to write the correct feeling words under each picture.

Word Bank		
glad	unhappy	pleased
sorry	sad	happy

_____

-          -

_____

-          -

_____

-          -

UNIT 9

Emotions

218

Name:_____

Feeling Words

Directions: Read the story. Then, write two different feelings the main character experiences in the story.

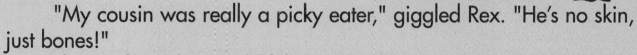

Yesterday, my friend Rex and I visited the museum. We were excited about seeing the new dinosaur display.

"Wow!" I yelled when I looked up at the tyrannosaurus skeleton.

"He's my distant cousin," Rex joked. "In fact, I was named after him!"

"My cousin was really a picky eater," giggled Rex. "He's no skin, just bones!"

That night, I dreamed of that tyrannosaurus. I imagined him sticking his head into my bedroom window. I was too frightened to scream. When he opened his huge mouth, I froze.

"Do you know what happened to me because I wouldn't take a bath?" thundered the dinosaur.

I shook my head.

"I became x-stinked!" he roared.

Now, I think that Rex and his dinosaur "cousin" must really be related. They both tell bad jokes!

_____   _____

-     -

UNIT 9

Name:_____

Feeling Words

Directions: Complete each sentence.

When I feel happy, I

- -

.

When I feel sad, I

- -

.

When I feel angry, I

- -

.

When I feel scared, I

- -

.

When I feel excited, I

- -

.

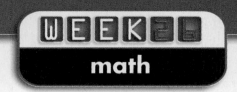

Time Words

Directions: Read about the days of the week. Then, answer the questions.

Do you know the names of the seven days of the week? Here they are: Sunday, Monday, Tuesday, Wednesday, Thursday, Friday, and Saturday.

1. What day comes after Thursday?

   -

2. What day comes before Tuesday?

   -

3. What day comes after Saturday?

   -

4. How many days are in each week?

   -

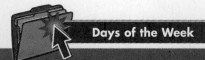
Days of the Week

UNIT 9

Name:_____

Words That Sound Like Noises

Onomatopoeia is the use of words that sound like the noises they represent. These words can make writing more interesting to read.

Example: The machine **clicked** and **whirred**, but it still did not work. My mother's favorite dish fell to the floor with a **crash**!

Directions: Draw a line from each word to the picture it describes.

ring-ring

meow

tick-tock

flutter

quack

boom

woof

splash

boing

achoo

UNIT 9

Name:_____

Figures of Speech

You can make sentences more interesting by using figures of speech. The following are four popular kinds of figures of speech.

Personification—gives human characteristics to things
   Example: The sun touched me with its warm fingers.
Hyperbole—great exaggeration
   Example: She is the happiest person in the universe.
Simile—compares two unlike things using **like** or **as**
   Example: He is as hungry as a horse.
Metaphor—suggests a comparison of two unlike things
   Example: The empty field was a desert.

Directions: Underline the figure of speech in each sentence. Then, write its name on the line.

1. The wind howled as the storm grew closer.

_____

2. The little lady nibbled at her lunch like a bird.

_____

3. Sarah's little sister was a doll in her new clothes.

_____

4. The leader said he would never sleep again.

_____

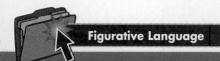
UNIT 9

Name:_____

Words That Are Palindromes

Directions: Use the words in the Word Bank to write the correct palindrome on each line.

Word Bank				
tot	dad	peep	pup	eye
sees	noon	bib	mom	ewe

1. Sound a chick makes

2. Midday

3. A napkin tied under a baby's chin

4. A little dog

5. Common name for father

6. Watches

7. A female sheep

8. A seeing organ

9. Short for mother

10. A small child

Name:_____

People Words

Word Bank			
Dr.	Miss	Mr.	Mrs.

Directions: Use the words in the Word Bank to write a correct title in each address.

1. _____ Tom Brown
   134 Main Street
   New Town, PA

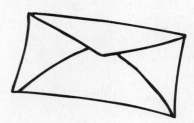

2. _____ Mary Wilson
   265 Greenwood Circle
   Dallas, TX

Mr. Larry Toad
1235 Lillypad Lane
Hopville, MI 49456

3. _____ Henry Boxer
   1567 West Avenue
   Springdale, VT

4. _____ Sally Smith
   901 Club Court
   Brownville, OR

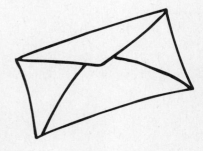

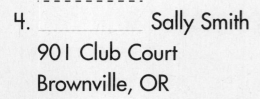
Abbreviations

225

UNIT 9

Name:_____

Feeling Words

Directions: Check the happy words in the top box. Then, find the checked words hidden in the puzzle. Look up, down, and sideways.

☐ jolly   ☐ sick   ☐ friendly
☐ pleased   ☐ scared   ☐ surprised
☐ lucky   ☐ proud   ☐ sorry
☐ mad   ☐ brave   ☐ excited

```
F  B  J  O  F  U  S  C  A
S  U  R  P  R  I  S  E  D
H  V  L  U  I  R  R  Y  E
N  A  P  L  E  A  S  E  D
G  L  J  K  N  C  P  M  O
Y  P  O  A  D  L  X  A  L
B  R  L  O  L  U  C  K  Y
K  O  L  T  Y  Z  Q  J  O
A  U  Y  U  O  E  T  P  L
K  D  B  R  A  V  E  S  I
E  X  C  I  T  E  D  E  M
```

UNIT 9

Name:_____

Feeling Words

Word Bank		
afraid	funny	happy
sad	sleepy	tired

Directions: Use the words in the Word Bank to write the correct feeling word in each sentence.

1. I am _____ when it is time to go to bed.

2. The clown is very _____ .

3. I am _____ of the dark.

4. When my dog ran away, I was _____ .

5. Running makes me _____ .

6. Everyone at the party was _____ .

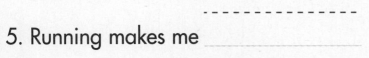
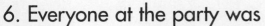
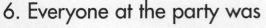

UNIT 9

Name:_____

Feeling Words

Directions: Use the words in the Word Bank to write the correct feeling word under each story.

Word Bank			
happy	excited	sad	mad

1. Andy and Sam were best friends. Sam and his family moved far away. How does Sam feel?

_____

- - - - - - - - - - - - - - - - - - -

2. Deana could not sleep. It was the night before her birthday party. How does Deana feel?

_____

- - - - - - - - - - - - - - - - - - -

3. Jacob let his baby brother play with his teddy bear. His brother lost the bear. How does Jacob feel?

_____

- - - - - - - - - - - - - - - - -

4. Kia picked flowers for her mom. Her mom smiled when she got them. How does Kia feel?

_____

- - - - - - - - - - - - - - - - - - -

UNIT 9

Name:_____

Unit 9 Review

Directions: Use the words in the Word Bank to write three examples of each kind of word.

Word Bank					
sad	they	no/know	Monday	fall	smell
sea/see	Miss	silly	hear	Thursday	right/write
cross	touch	pleased	land	you	Saturday

Homophones

1. _____

2. _____

3. _____

Homonyms

1. _____

2. _____

3. _____

People

1. _____

2. _____

3. _____

Senses

1. _____

2. _____

3. _____

Days of the Week

1. _____

2. _____

3. _____

Feelings

1. _____

2. _____

3. _____

UNIT 9

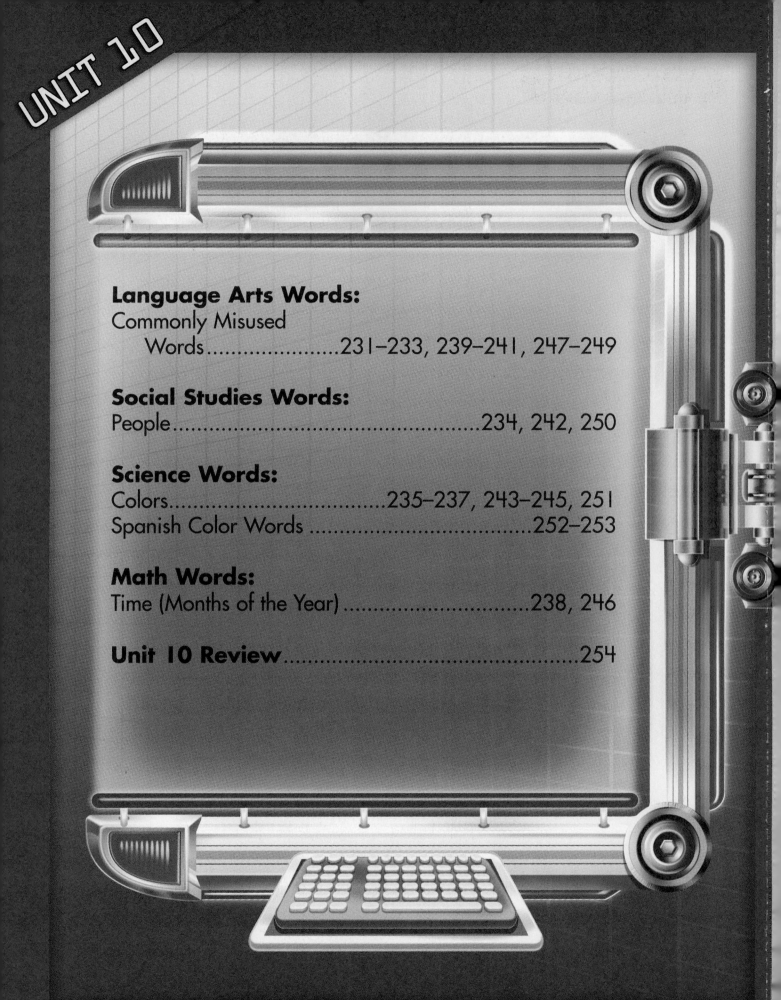

UNIT 10

Commonly Misused Words

The word **can** means **am able to** or **to be able to**.
Examples: I **can** do that for you.
              Can you do that for me?

The word **may** means **be allowed to** or **permitted to**. **May** is used to ask or to give permission. **May** can also mean **might** or **perhaps**.
Examples: **May** I be excused?
              You **may** sit here.

Directions: Write **can** or **may** to complete each sentence. The first one is done for you.

1. **May** Can/May I help you?

2. _____ He's smart. He can/may do it himself.

3. _____ When can/may I have my dessert?

4. _____ He can/may speak French fluently.

5. _____ You can/may use my pencil.

6. _____ Can/May my friend stay for dinner?

7. _____ You can/may leave when your report is finished.

8. _____ Can/May you hear the dog barking?

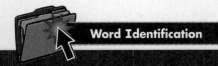

Name:_____

Commonly Misused Words

The word **sit** means **to rest**.
Examples: Please **sit** here!
Will you **sit** by me?

The word **set** means **to put** or **place something**.
Examples: **Set** your purse there.
Set the dishes on the table.

Directions: Write **sit** or **set** to complete each sentence. The first one is done for you.

1. **sit**   Would you please sit/set down here?

2. _____ You can sit/set the groceries there.

3. _____ She is a person who cannot sit/set still.

4. _____ Where did you sit/set your new shoes?

5. _____ They decided to sit/set together during the movie.

6. _____ He sit/set the greasy pan in the sink.

7. _____ She sit/set the candles on the cake.

8. _____ Get ready! Get sit/set! Go!

UNIT 10

Name:_____

Commonly Misused Words

The word **they're** means **they are**.
Examples: **They're** our very best friends!
Ask them if **they're** coming over tomorrow.

The word **their** shows ownership.
Examples: **Their** dog is friendly.
It is **their** bicycle.

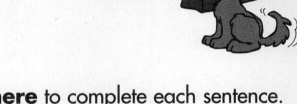

The word **there** shows place or direction.
Examples: Look over **there**.
There it is!

Directions: Write **they're**, **their**, or **there** to complete each sentence. The first one is done for you.

1. There   They're/Their/There is the sweater I want!

2. _____ Do you believe they're/their/there stories?

3. _____ Be they're/their/there by one o'clock.

4. _____ Have you met they're/their/there mother?

5. _____ Do you like they're/their/there new car?

6. _____ They're/Their/There friendly to everyone.

7. _____ Did she say they're/their/there ready to go?

8. _____ Is anyone they're/their/there?

UNIT 10

Name:_____

People Words

Directions: Trace and write the word. Complete each sentence with the word. Then, draw a picture of how you play.

play play

I can _____ .

I like to _____ .

How do I _____ ?

Name:_____

Color Words

Directions: Trace and write the color words. The first one is done for you.

orange   orange

blue

green

yellow

red

brown

UNIT 10

Name:_____

Color Words

Directions: Complete each sentence with the correct color word. Put a period at the end of each sentence. The first one is done for you.

| green tree | blue bike | yellow chick | red ball |

1. The baby  is  **yellow** ⊙

2. This  is ☐

3. My is big and ☐

4. My sister's  is ☐

UNIT 10

Name:_____

Color Words

Directions: Complete the puzzle about colors.

```
                          y
  b [ ][ ]  e
                          l
          b  l [ ][ ]
      g [■] o
  b [ ][ ]  w [ ]
              
      r [ ]
```

UNIT 10

Name:_____

Time Words

The months of the year begin with capital letters.

Directions: Use the words in the Word Bank to write the months of the year in order on the calendar.

Word Bank					
January	December	April	May	October	June
September	February	July	March	November	August

- - - - - - - - - - - -	- - - - - - - - - - - -
- - - - - - - - - - - -	- - - - - - - - - - - -
- - - - - - - - - - - -	- - - - - - - - - - - -
- - - - - - - - - - - -	- - - - - - - - - - - -
- - - - - - - - - - - -	- - - - - - - - - - - -
- - - - - - - - - - - -	- - - - - - - - - - - -

UNIT 10

Months

238

Name:_____

Commonly Misused Words

Use the word **good** to describe a person, place, or thing.

Example: He is a **good** teacher.

Use the word **well** to describe how something is done or how someone is feeling.

Example: She is not feeling **well**.

Directions: Trace and write the commonly misused words. Then, complete each sentence with the correct word.

good

well

1. I can throw the ball _____.

2. She is _____ at drawing.

UNIT 10

Name:_____

Commonly Misused Words

Here is Sue. She is a **good** skater.
She skates **well**.

When you describe a person, a place, or a thing, use the word **good**. When you describe how something is done, use the word **well**.

Directions: Circle **good** or **well** to complete each sentence.

1. Andrew is a **good**, **well** singer.

2. Wanda dances **good**, **well**.

3. Antonio writes stories **good**, **well**.

4. Tim is a **good**, **well** reader.

5. Carmen is a **good**, **well** cook.

6. Helen paints **good**, **well**.

7. Doug adds numbers **good**, **well**.

Name:_____

Commonly Misused Words

The word **its** shows ownership.
Example: Its leaves are green.

The word **it's** means **it is**.
Example: It's better to be early than late.

Directions: Trace and write the commonly misused words. Then, complete each sentence with the correct word.

its

it's

1. The cat is licking _____ paws.

2. _____ a beautiful day outside.

Name:_____

People Words

Directions: Trace and write the word. Complete each sentence with the word. Then, draw a picture of how you work.

work work -

- -

I can _____ .

- -

I like to _____ .

- -

How do I _____ ?

UNIT 10

Name:_____

Color Words

Directions: Write three sentences that tell about this picture. Use a color word in each one. Begin each sentence with a capital letter and end it with a period.

1. _____

_____

2. _____

_____

3. _____

UNIT 10

Name:_____

Color Words

Directions: Use the words in the Word Bank to complete each sentence with the correct color word.

Word Bank		
yellow	white	blue
green	black	red

_____
- - - - - - - - - - - - - - - - - -

The sky is _____ .

_____   _____
- - - - - - - - - - - - - - -   - - - - - - - - - - - - - - - - -

Grass is _____ . The sun is _____ .

_____
- - - - - - - - - - - - - - - -

An apple is _____ .

_____   _____
- - - - - - - - - - - - - - -   - - - - - - - - - - - - - - -

A zebra is _____ and _____ .

Directions: Write **ay**, **i**, or **o** to make a color word.

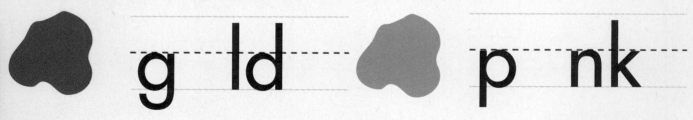

g ld   p nk

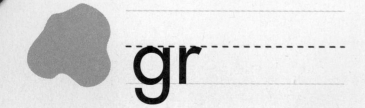

gr

UNIT 10

Name: _____

Color Words

Directions: Use the words in the Word Bank to complete the puzzles about colors.

Across

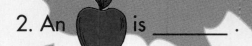

1. A 🥕 is _____.

Down

2. An 🍎 is _____.

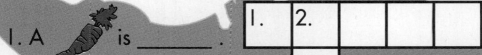

Across

2. 🍇 are _____.

Down

1. An 🐘 is _____.

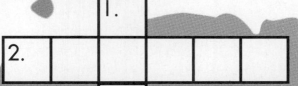

Across

2. A 🍁 is _____.

Down

1. A 🪵 is _____.

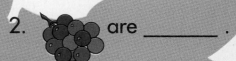

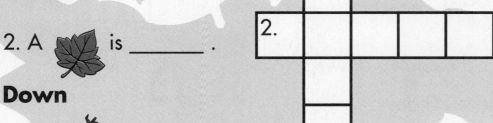

Word Bank					
brown	orange	purple	green	red	gray

Name:_____

Time Words

There are 12 months in a year. The first month is January. The last month is December. Some months have 31 days. Some months have 30 days. February is the shortest month with 28 days.

Directions: Write 1 to 12 in the boxes to put the months in order. The first one is done for you.

☐ February
☐ April
☐ May
☐ July
☐ October
☐ August
[1] January
☐ December
☐ March
☐ September
☐ June
☐ November

Directions: Write the correct answer.

first month _____ last month _____

Directions: Circle the correct answer.

1. Some months have 30 days.   Yes   No

2. Some months have 31 days.   Yes   No

3. February is the longest month.   Yes   No

4. February has 28 days.   Yes   No

UNIT 10

Months

246

Name:_____

Commonly Misused Words

The word **this** is a describing word that refers to things that are near. **This** always describes a single person, place, or thing.
Example: I will buy **this** coat.

The word **these** is also a describing word that refers to things that are near. **These** always describes more than one person, place, or thing.
Example: I will buy **these** flowers.

Directions: Write **this** or **these** to complete each sentence. The first one is done for you.

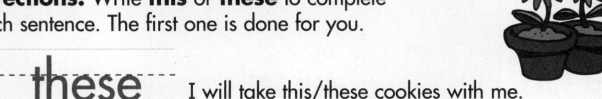

1. these _____ I will take this/these cookies with me.

2. _____ Do you want this/these seeds?

3. _____ Do it this/these way!

4. _____ Did you open this/these window?

5. _____ Will you carry this/these books for me?

6. _____ This/These pans are hot!

7. _____ Do you think this/these light is too bright?

8. _____ Are this/these boots yours?

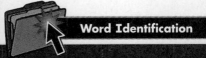

Word Identification

247

UNIT 10

Name:_____

Commonly Misused Words

The word **your** shows possession.
Examples: Is that **your** book?
I visited **your** class.

The word **you're** means **you are**.
Examples: **You're** doing well on that painting.
If **you're** going to pass the test, you should study.

Directions: Write **your** or **you're** to complete each sentence. The first one is done for you.

1. You're   Your/You're the best friend I have!

2. _____   Your/You're brother came to see me.

3. _____   If your/you're going, you'd better hurry!

4. _____   It's none of your/you're business!

5. _____   Your/You're kidding!

6. _____   I thought your/you're report was great!

7. _____   He thinks your/you're wonderful!

8. _____   What is your/you're first choice?

Word Identification   248

UNIT 10

Name:_____

Commonly Misused Words

Directions: Help the coach get to the castle. Complete each sentence with the correct word.

The road _ _ _ _ _ _ _ _ _ _ bumpy.
       is, are

Sara ate _ _ _ _ _ _ _ _ _ _ muffin.
       a, an

The horses _ _ _ _ _ _ _ _ _ _ running.
       is, are

Colin is a _ _ _ _ _ _ _ _ _ _ _ _ _ _ rider.
       good, well

José prints _ _ _ _ _ _ _ _ _ _ _ _ _ _ .
       good, well

The coach _ _ _ _ _ _ _ _ _ _ near the castle.
       is, are

UNIT 10

Name:_____

People Words

Directions: List at least 15 different kinds of people you might see while out on a walk. Go on a walk with an adult. When you spot people you listed, check them off of your list. Some suggestions are: police officer, truck driver, jogger, etc.

MY PEOPLE WATCH LIST

UNIT 10

Name:_____

Color Words

Directions: Use the words in the Word Bank to find the color words. Look up, down, and sideways.

o	r	a	n	g	e	b	d	c	a	e	g	i	k	r	z	t
p	x	h	o	e	b	u	n	w	n	f	a	d	f	e	q	x
i	l	m	n	b	l	v	c	x	z	a	s	f	g	d	h	a
n	y	u	i	o	u	r	e	w	q	t	p	w	h	i	t	e
k	g	r	a	y	e	x	p	b	n	v	m	x	k	y	u	p
b	u	d	r	u	g	t	u	b	r	o	w	n	m	e	n	o
l	a	s	d	m	r	r	r	v	n	e	t	y	w	l	l	h
a	b	d	f	g	e	h	p	j	k	m	u	z	m	l	n	e
c	g	h	k	o	e	i	l	e	w	n	l	v	f	o	g	n
k	s	d	u	e	n	l	e	j	o	m	c	s	x	w	y	w

Word Bank

blue   black   brown
yellow   red   pink
orange   gray   green
purple   white

Color the squares you circled blue. What did you find? _____

   © 2007 School Specialty Publishing

Name:_____

Spanish Color Words

Directions: Use the words in the Word Bank to write the color words in Spanish on the rainbow. Then, color the rainbow.

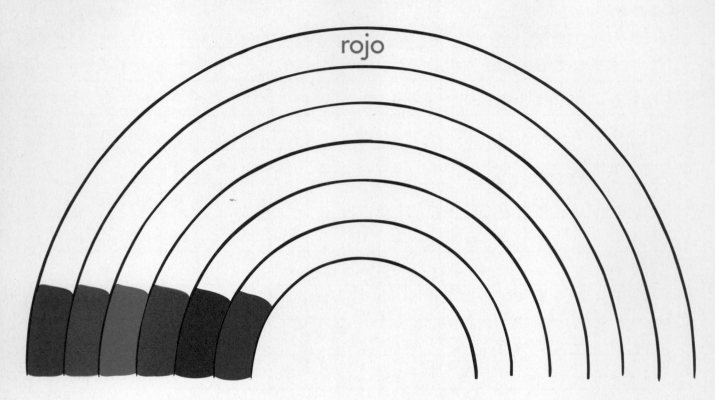

rojo

Word Bank

red – rojo   blue – azul

orange – naranja   green – verde

yellow – amarillo   purple – morado

UNIT 10

Name:_____

Spanish Color Words

- ● red – rojo (rō–hō)
- ● orange – naranja (nah–rahn–ha)
- ● yellow – amarillo (ah–mah–rē–yō)
- ● green – verde (ver–dā)
- ● blue – azul (ah–zool)
- ● purple – morado (mō-rah-dō)
- ● black – negro (nā–grō)
- ○ white – blanco (blāhn–kō)
- ● brown – marrón (mah-rōn)

Directions: Read each color word. Say each color word in Spanish. Then, write the Spanish word next to the English word. Color each crayon to match the color word.

black _____

blue _____

green _____

brown _____

orange _____

red _____

purple _____

white _____

yellow _____

UNIT 10

Name:_____

Unit 10 Review

Directions: Circle the correct word for each sentence. Write it on the line.

1. He is a _____ student.   good   well

2. _____ hard to sit still when it is sunny outside.   Its   It's

3. Is she _____ sister?   your   you're

4. You may _____ your book bag on the table.   sit   set

5. I like to visit _____ house.   their   there

6. _____ is the shortest month.   May   February

Directions: Read each color word. Then, circle the two things that the color word describes.

1. **azul**	sky	cow	water
2. **naranja**	carrot	pumpkin	grapes
3. **verde**	leaf	elephant	grass
4. amarillo	sun	horse	lemon

Name: Shelbi

Words You Use Often

Directions: Trace and write the commonly used words.

the

are

for

was

said

you

UNIT 11

Name:_____

Words You Use Often

Directions: Use the words in the Word Bank to complete the story.

Word Bank					
You	for	was	said	the	are

I _____ late for _____ party!

" _____

_____ must hurry," _____ my mom.

Your friends _____ waiting _____ you.

Directions: A **contraction** is two words joined into one shorter word. Use the words in the Word Bank to write the correct contraction on each line.

Word Bank	
are not	= aren't
was not	= wasn't
you are	= you're

was not _____   you are _____   are not _____

Sight Words

UNIT 11

Name:_____

Words You Use Often

Directions: Draw a line to match the beginning letter of each word with the rest of its letters.

re   or

aid   ou

as   he

Directions: Trace and write the math words.

add   many   all

Directions: Write each math word below its meaning.

every one   a lot   sum

Name:_____

Job Words

Directions: Use the words in the Word Bank to complete each sentence with the correct job word.

Word Bank		
pilot	farmer	doctor
builder	plumber	teacher

A _____ helps us learn new things.

A _____ helps people get well.

A _____ flies planes many places.

A _____ plants and grows crops.

A _____ fixes many leaky pipes.

A _____ builds new buildings.

Careers

259

© 2007 School Specialty Publishing

Name:_____

Magnet Words

A magnet can **pull** another magnet. Or a magnet can **push** another magnet.

Directions: Trace and write the magnet words.

pull   pull- - - - - - - - - - - - - - - -

push   push- - - - - - - - - - - - - - - -

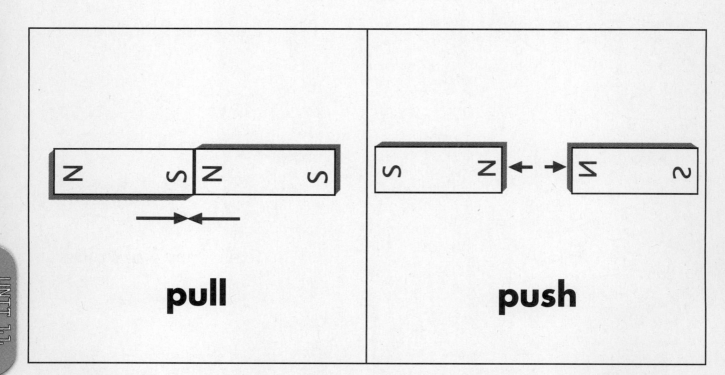

pull   push

Name:_____

Magnet Words

Every magnet has a north pole and a south pole.

When a north pole and a south pole are next to each other, they **pull** together.

S	N		S	N

When two north poles or two south poles are next to each other, they **push** apart.

S	N		N	S

Directions: Write **push** or **pull** to tell what each pair of magnets will do.

```
N
S
―――
S
N
```

```
N
S
―――
N
S
```

_____ _____ _____

- - - - - - - - - - - - - - - - - - - - - - - - - - - - - - - - - - - -

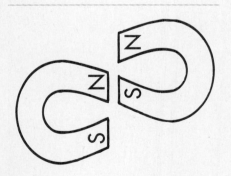

```
S
N
―――
N
S
```

_____ _____ _____

- - - - - - - - - - - - - - - - - - - - - - - - - - - - - - - - - - - -

UNIT 11

Name:_____

Magnet Words

Directions: Trace and write the words. Then, make lists of the things in your bedroom that will and will not stick to a magnet. (Do not try your magnet on anything electronic.)

magnet magnet ----------------------------

Magnets stick to:	Magnets do not stick to:

UNIT 11

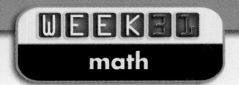

Name:_____

Money Words

Directions: Read about coins. Then, answer the questions.

You can use coins to buy things. Some coins are worth more than others. Do you know these coins? A penny is worth one cent. A nickel is worth five cents. A dime is worth 10 cents. A quarter is worth 25 cents.

1. What can you use coins to do?

_____

- -

_____

2. How are coins different?

_____

- -

_____

Directions: Number the coins in order from the one that is worth the least to the one that is worth the most. Then, write how many cents each coin is worth.

 nickel ☐    penny ☐   dime ☐

- - - - - - - - - -   - - - - - - - - - -   - - - - - - - - - -
cents   cent   cents

UNIT 11

Name:_____

Words You Use Often

Directions: Use the words in the Word Bank to write about a time when you had to count things.

Word Bank				
the	for	said	add	all
are	was	you	many	

_____

- -

_____

- -

_____

- -

Directions: Use the words in the Word Bank to write the commonly used words in ABC order.

Word Bank		
the	for	said
are	was	you

1. _____   3. _____   5. _____

_____   _____   _____

- -

2. _____   4. _____   6. _____

UNIT 11

Name:_____

Words You Use Often

Directions: Trace and write the commonly used words.

do

have

come

her

they

want

UNIT 11

Name:_____

Words You Use Often

Directions: Use the words in the Word Bank to complete each sentence with the correct commonly used word.

Word Bank					
her	come	want	do	have	they

I _____ two friends who _____

_____

to play. I'll ask Mom if I need to _____ some work

_____

first. Then, I'll ask _____ if _____

_____

can _____ over.

Name:_____

Job Words

Directions: Use the words in the Word Bank to complete the puzzle about jobs.

Across
4. A person who paints.
6. A person who cooks food.
7. A person who sails.
9. A person who makes you well.

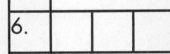

Down
1. A person who makes you laugh.
2. A person who bakes cakes.
3. A person who farms.
5. A person who teaches.
8. A person who acts.

Word Bank

doctor	baker	teacher
clown	farmer	actor
sailor	painter	cook

UNIT 11

Name:_____

Words About Simple Machines

A **lever** is a simple machine used to lift or move things. It has two parts. The **arm** is the part that moves. The **fulcrum** supports the arm but does not move.

Directions: Label the parts of this lever.

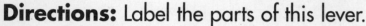
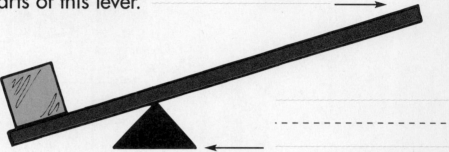

Directions: The letters in each word are mixed up. Unscramble the letters to write the name of each kind of lever correctly.

velosh

_____

mrahem

_____

orbom

_____

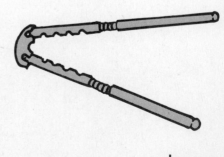

tun   reckarc

_____

Name:_____

Words About Simple Machines

Directions: Use the words in the Word Bank to name the simple machine in each picture. Then, you will find the answer to this question: What do machines use to work?

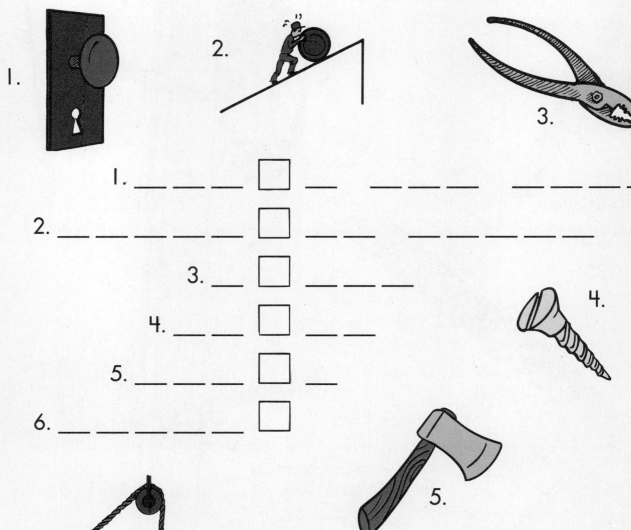

1.

2.

3.

4.

5.

6.

1. __ __ __ [ ] __ __ __ __ __ __ __ __

2. __ __ __ __ __ [ ] __ __ __ __ __ __ __ __ __

3. __ [ ] __ __ __ __

4. __ __ __ [ ] __ __ __

5. __ __ __ [ ] __

6. __ __ __ __ [ ]

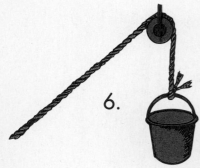

Word Bank

wheel and axle	inclined plane	screw
wedge	lever	pulley

UNIT 11

Name:_____

Words About Simple Machines

Directions: Use the words in the Word Bank to write the correct tools under each simple machine.

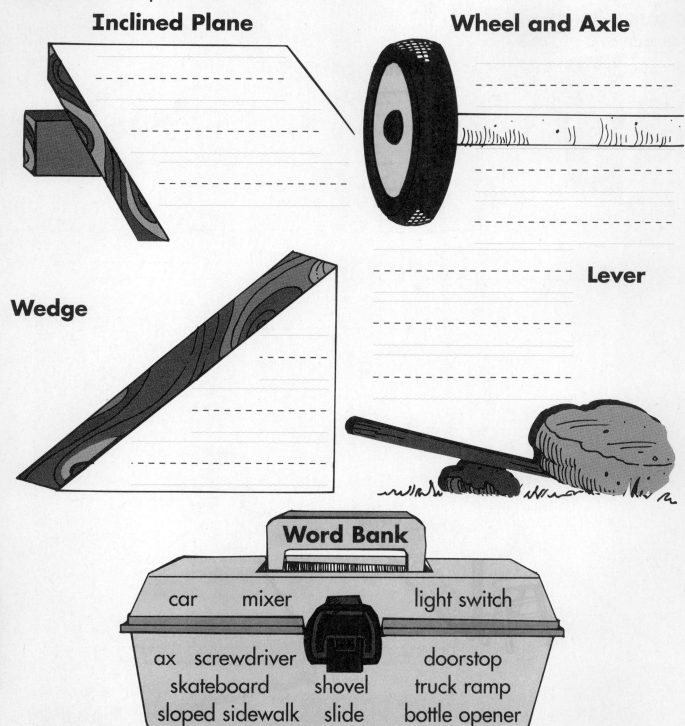

Inclined Plane

Wheel and Axle

Wedge

Lever

Word Bank

car   mixer   light switch

ax   screwdriver   doorstop
skateboard   shovel   truck ramp
sloped sidewalk   slide   bottle opener

Simple Machines

270

© 2007 School Specialty Publishing

UNIT 11

Name:_____

Words About Fractions

The word **equal** means **the same**. The word **unequal** means **not the same**.

Directions: Circle each shape that is divided into equal parts. Draw an **X** on each shape that is divided into unequal parts.

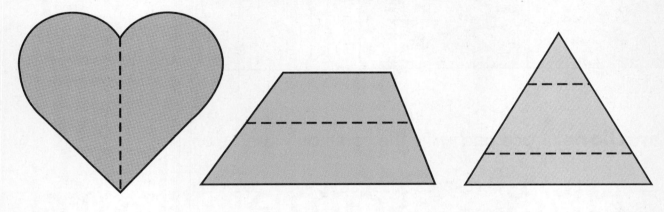

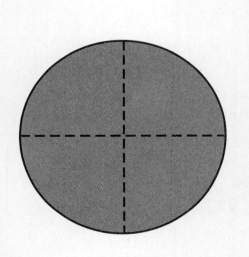

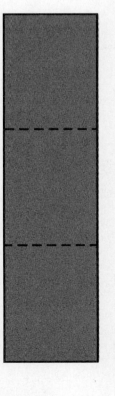

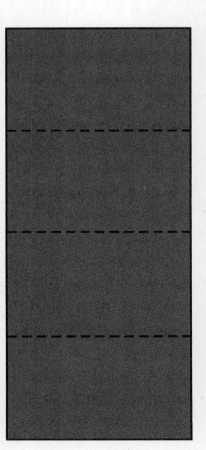

UNIT 11

Name:_____

Words You Use Often

Directions: Use the words in the Word Bank to find the commonly used words. Look up, down, and sideways.

r	w	a	n	t	c	p
t	r	e	c	d	o	t
n	k	o	c	e	m	h
t	r	h	a	v	e	e
h	e	r	w	d	e	y

Word Bank

come	do	have
her	they	want

Directions: Trace and write the commonly used words.

and   some   here

Directions: Write the missing letter to complete each word.

nd   som

h re

Sight Words

272

UNIT 11

Name:_____

Words You Use Often

Directions: Do you like people to visit you at home? Use the words in the Word Bank to write about your favorite visitors.

Word Bank				
do	come	they	and	here
have	her	want	some	

Directions: Circle the word in each pair that is not spelled correctly.

1. they   thay

2. dou   do

3. have   hav

4. cume   come

5. hur   her

6. want   wonte

Name: _____

Overused Words

It is easy to use certain words again and again. Try giving "tired" words a break!

Directions: Use the words in the Word Bank to replace the tired words in the paragraph. Rewrite the paragraph.

Word Bank			
gorgeous	pleasant	friendly	countless

Last Friday, our class had a <u>nice</u> time at the Tropical Gardens. We saw <u>many</u> flowers, trees, and plants. The exotic birds were <u>beautiful</u>. We had a <u>good</u> guide who let us take pictures.

Name:_____

Job Words

Directions: Draw a picture of what you might look like when you grow up. Then, write what you want to be when you grow up.

When I grow up, I want to be a

- -

- -

because . . .

- -

- -

- -

- -

UNIT 11

Name:_____

Words About Simple Machines

Directions: Tyrone and Kim have a list of jobs to do. Help them pick the right tool for each job. Draw a line from each job to the correct tool.

1. What will help Kim raise the flag up the flagpole?

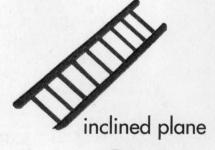
inclined plane

2. What will Tyrone use to help him get the cat out of the tree?

pulley

3. What will Kim use to carry sand to her new sandbox?

lever

4. What will Tyrone use to get the nail out of the board?

screw

5. What will Kim use to hang the mirror on her bedroom door?

wheel and axle

6. What will Tyrone use to slice the turkey?

wedge

Name:_____

Words About Simple Machines

Directions: Color and cut out each simple machine. Then, glue each one in the correct place.

Screw	**Lever**	**Pulley**
Wedge	**Wheel and Axle**	**Inclined Plane**

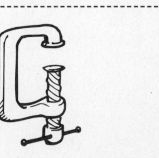

UNIT 11

Page left blank for cutting activity.

UNIT 11

Name:_____

Unit 11 Review

Directions: An inventor is a person who invents or makes new things. Pretend that you are an inventor. Draw a simple machine. Then, write two sentences to explain how your machine works.

UNIT 11

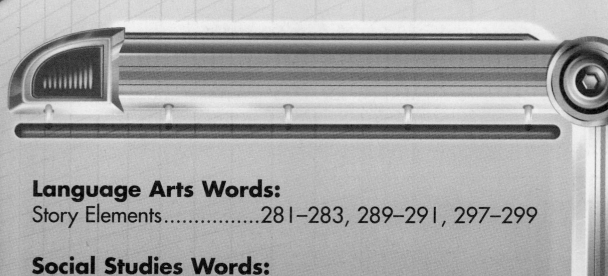

UNIT 12

Name:_____

Story Words

Story elements are the parts of a story that make up its beginning, middle, and end. A good story will contain these story elements:

Title — the name of a story that gives a clue as to what the story is about
Setting — where and when the story takes place
Characters — the people, animals, or objects that the story is about
Plot — the sequence of events in a story that create a problem
Climax — the most thrilling part of the story where the problem is either solved or the plot thickens
Resolution — how the characters solve the story problem
Conclusion — what happens to the characters in the end

Directions: Write the letter of the definition that matches the story element.

1. _____ Setting

2. _____ Characters

3. _____ Plot

4. _____ Climax

5. _____ Resolution

6. _____ Conclusion

a. the way a story ends

b. the changing point of a story—often the most exciting part of the story

c. the series of events in a story involving a problem

d. the place and time

e. people or animals in the story

f. the way in which the problems are solved

Name:_____

Story Words

A **character** is the **person**, **animal**, or **object** that a story is about. You can't have a story without a character.

Characters are usually people, but sometimes they are animals, aliens, or even objects that come to life. You can have many characters in a story.

Directions: Read the story. Circle the three characters named in the story.

Rorie the Reader!

Rorie loved to read. Rorie would read everything she could find: books, magazines, even cereal boxes!

She loved to read so much that she would always carry books in her bag in case she had a free second to read.

Rorie had blond hair and was very pale. Her mom would say, "Rorie, please go outside and play. You need to get some sunshine."

Rorie would answer, "Do I have to, Mom? I would rather read."

One day, Rorie's teacher said to her mom, "I have never seen a girl who loves to read so much. You are very lucky to have a daughter like Rorie." From then on, Rorie's mom let her read whenever she wanted.

Name:_____

Story Words

The **events** in a story describe all the things that happen.

Directions: Read each problem. Write two events that tell what happens.

1. Heavy black clouds darken the sky. Travis is walking home without an umbrella.

   _____
   _____
   _____
   _____
   _____

2. Marcella worked very hard on her book report last night. This morning, she was in such a rush to get to school that she left her report on the table at home.

   _____
   _____
   _____
   _____

3. Ben's school is having a fundraiser. In order to win the scooter, Ben will have to sell 50 magazine subscriptions.

   _____
   _____
   _____
   _____

Story Elements

283

UNIT 12

Name:_____

Clothing Words

Directions: Trace and write the clothing words. The first one is done for you.

shirt   shirt

pants

jacket

socks

shoes

dress

hat

Name: _____

Words About Things That Go

Directions: Trace and write the names of the things that go. Then, color the pictures. The first one is done for you.

 car   car

 truck

 train

 bike

 plane

UNIT 12

Name:_____

Words About Things That Go

Directions: Write the missing letter or letters for each word. The first one is done for you.

car   car

pl_ne   __ane

b_k_   _i_e

tr__n   __ain

__uck   tr_ck

Transportation

286

Name:_____

Words About Things That Go

Directions: The letters in each word are mixed up. Unscramble the letters to write each word correctly. The first one is done for you.

rac   car

aitrn   _____

eplna   _____

kibe   _____

ckutr   _____

Name:_____

Weight Words

Directions: Read about weight. Then, circle the correct answers.

Weight is a measurement that tells how heavy something is. Almost everything in your room can be weighed.

You can describe weight in **pounds** or **ounces**. You can describe weight in **kilograms** or **grams**.

Where have you seen weight? Maybe you have seen weight on a box of cereal. Food is sometimes weighed in **ounces** or **grams**. Maybe the nurse weighed you at the doctor's office. People often measure their own weight in **pounds** or **kilograms**.

1. Weight tells how _____ something is.
   a. long
   b. wide
   c. heavy

2. Which can be used to show weight?
   a. meters
   b. grams
   c. liters

3. How are people usually weighed?
   a. miles
   b. gallons
   c. pounds

4. How is food sometimes weighed?
   a. ounces
   b. meters
   c. inches

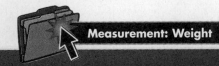

Name:_____

Story Words

Stories have a setting and a plot. The **setting** tells where and when the story takes place. The **plot** tells what happened.

Directions: Trace and write the story words. Then, complete each sentence with the correct story word.

setting  setting

plot plot

Michael, Sam and Dominic were best friends. They ate lunch together. At recess, they swung on the swings together. On the swings, Michael said, "Come to my house to play after school." Dominic thought Michael was looking at Sam. He waited for Michael to ask him, too, but Michael didn't. All afternoon, Dominic felt sad. When the bell rang, he started to go home.
"Where are you going?" Michael called. "I wanted you both to come to my house." With a big smile, Dominic ran to join Michael and Sam.

1. In the story's _____, Michael invited his friends to play.

2. The jungle gym is the _____ for the story.

Story Words

Every story has a setting. The **setting** is the place where the story happens.

Directions: Think of a place that you know well. It could be your room, your kitchen, your backyard, your classroom, or an imaginary place. Think about what you see, hear, smell, taste, or feel in that place. Brainstorm some words and ideas that describe the place. Write your ideas below.

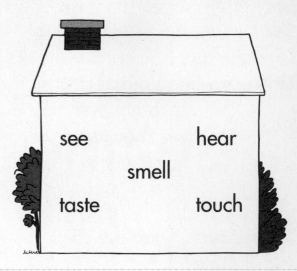

Story Elements

Name:_____

Story Words

The **setting** is the place where the story happens. The setting is also the time when the story happens. Does it take place at night? On a sunny day? In the future? During the winter?

Time can be: time of day
a holiday
a season of the year
a time in history
a time in the future

Directions: Read the story. Then, answer the questions.

Pizza Night!

Last Tuesday, we made pizzas for dinner. We made mini-pizzas out of pita bread, tomato sauce, mozzarella cheese, and vegetable toppings. Then, my mom put our "M.P.s" (mini-pizzas) into the oven for the cheese to melt. Mmm-m-m! Delicious!

1. What time of day did this story take place? _____

2. What day of the week did this story take place? _____

3. What happened in the story?

_____

_____

_____

Name: _____

Clothing Words

Directions: The words by each picture are mixed up. Use them to write a sentence that tells about the picture. Begin each sentence with a capital letter and end it with a period.

Example: is shirt a drying.

A shirt is drying.

1. ties his shoes he

2. red wear I a jacket

3. blue are pants his

Name:_____

Words About Things That Go

Directions: These sentences tell about things that go. Complete each sentence with the correct word. Use the pictures to help you.

Example:

The _____ car _____ is in the garage.

_____

1. The _____ was at the farm.

_____

2. My _____ had a flat tire.

_____

3. The _____ flew high.

_____

4. The _____ went fast.

Transportation

293

UNIT 12

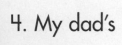

Name: _____

Words About Things That Go

Directions: Complete the names of the things that go. Then, draw a line from the first part of the sentence to the part that completes it. Put a period at the end of each sentence.

Example: _____

The blue **bike** ------------------

is in the bike rack •

1. The **c** - - - - - - - - - - - - - - -

carries dirt ☐

2. Bob's **t** - - - - - - - - - - - - - - -

is purple ☐

3. The **t** - - - - - - - - - - - - - - -

flies high ☐

4. My dad's **p** - - - - - - - - - - - - - - -

is full ☐

UNIT 12

Name:_____

Words About Things That Go

Directions: Draw a line from the first part of the sentence to the part that completes it. Put a period at the end of each sentence. The first one is done for you.

1. The car

2. The truck

3. The train

4. The bike

5. The plane

carries toys ☐

is being washed ⊡

takes off ☐

is red ☐

has wheels ☐

Name:_____

Weight Words

Directions: Read each question. Then, circle the correct answer.

Which weighs **MORE**?	Which weighs **LESS**?
toasted oat cereal or popcorn	toasted oat cereal or beans
Which weighs **MORE**?	Which weighs **LESS**?
marbles or beans	marbles or beans
Which weighs **MORE**?	Which weighs **LESS**?
macaroni or paper clips	popcorn or paper clips
Which weighs **MORE**?	Which weighs **LESS**?
pebbles or marbles	macaroni or pebbles

UNIT 12

Name:_____

Story Words

The **solution** in a story is the way the problem is solved. Sometimes, the main character solves the problem. Sometimes, the problem is solved in other ways.

Directions: Draw a line from each story to its solution.

Sara and Melody are enjoying fishing from a boat. Suddenly, the boat starts filling with water. They search frantically to find where the boat is leaking. They discover a hole in the bottom. A shark must have bitten the bottom of the boat!

Peter and Tyrone are camping. They set up the tent and settle into their sleeping bags. A huge thing thunders through the tent roaring, and then the tent collapses. Could it be a bear? Peter gets out to investigate.

Today is the big game against the Blue Dragons. Nina wakes up and gets out of bed. She falls straight to the floor. Looking down, she finds her feet have turned into flippers.

It is just the wind from an approaching storm. The boys get out and fix the tent.

She drinks a magic potion that changes her flippers back into feet.

The girls call for help on their two-way radio.

Name:_____

Story Words

In some paragraphs, the order of the sentences is very important. **Transition words**, such as **first**, **next**, **after**, **then**, **finally**, and **last**, offer clues to help show the sequence of the sentences.

Directions: Read the story. Circle the transition words.

My brother is convinced that he makes the best apple pie in the world! He claims he has tried over 100 different recipes and has found the perfect one.

First, he says it's all about the apples. He is convinced you must use only hand-picked Granny Smith apples. Next, you must carefully slice all the apples. After you have sliced them, you must add white and brown sugar, nutmeg, lemon juice, and butter. Then, you need to preheat the oven while you make the crust.

Finally, when the crust is ready, you put the apples in the crust and bake it at 350 degrees for a perfect apple pie!

Name:_____

Story Words

A **fiction** book is a book about things that are made up or not true. Fantasy books are fiction. A **nonfiction** book is about things that have really happened. Books can be classified into more types within these two groups.

Mystery – a book that has clues that lead to solving a problem or mystery

Biography – a book about a real person's life

Poetry – a book that has a collection of poems, which may or may not rhyme

Fantasy – a book about things that cannot really happen

Sports – a book about different sports or sports figures

Travel – a book about going to other places

Directions: Write **mystery**, **biography**, **poetry**, **fantasy**, **sports**, or **travel** next to each title.

1. *The Life of Helen Keller* _____

2. *Let's Go to Mexico!* _____

3. *The Case of the Missing Doll* _____

4. *How to Play Golf* _____

5. *Turtle Soup and Other Poems* _____

6. *Fred's Flying Saucer* _____

Name:_____

Clothing Words

Directions: Complete each sentence with a clothing word. Use the pictures to help you. Put a period at the end of each sentence.

Example:

Mike is wearing a ------ hat ------ .

1. Put on your socks before your _____ ☐

2. When it's cold wear a _____ ☐

3. The little girl liked to wear a pink _____ ☐

4. He wore jeans with the _____ ☐

5. The man wore a suit coat and _____ ☐

6. The clown wore long, striped _____ ☐

UNIT 12

Name:_____

Words About Things That Go

Directions: Read the story.

Sarah built a car for a race. Sarah's car has wheels, a steering wheel, and a place to sit just like the family car. It doesn't have a motor, a key, or a gas pedal. Sarah came in second in last year's race. This year, she hopes to win the race.

Directions: Write **S** beside the things Sarah's car has that are like things the family car has. Write **D** beside the things that are different.

1. _____

steering wheel

2. _____

motor

3. _____

gas pedal

4. _____

seat

5. _____

wheels

Name:_____

Words About Things That Go

Directions: Read about boats. Then, answer the questions.

See the boats! They float on water. Some boats have sails. The wind moves the sails. It makes the boats go. Many people name their sailboats. They paint the name on the side of the boat.

1. What makes sailboats move? _____

_____

_____

2. Where do sailboats float? _____

_____

_____

3. What would you name a sailboat? _____

Name:_____

Words About Things That Go

Directions: Find and circle the words from the Word Bank. Look across and down.

Word Bank

monorail	trains	cable cars	schoolbus	tram
airplane	bus	elevator	ship	truck
boat	cab	escalator	subway	van
car	jet	helicopter	taxi	

s	g	a	b	g	t	h	o	v	i	w	a	k	l	o	h
f	t	r	u	c	k	e	l	e	v	a	t	o	r	n	e
s	s	h	i	p	e	s	c	a	l	a	t	o	r	b	c
u	b	o	a	t	c	a	b	l	e	c	a	r	s	h	w
p	t	a	x	i	s	c	h	o	o	l	b	u	s	e	g
x	t	r	a	i	n	s	a	i	r	p	l	a	n	e	v
o	t	r	a	m	h	e	l	i	c	o	p	t	e	r	a
f	s	u	b	w	a	y	m	o	n	o	r	a	i	l	n
n	o	s	b	u	s	o	e	f	a	c	a	b	t	p	s
y	n	e	c	a	r	u	n	f	t	j	e	t	o	i	e

Color the squares you circled yellow.

- -

What did you find?

UNIT 12

Name:_____

Unit 12 Review

Directions: Write a story about a place that you would like to visit.
Think about:

- How you will get there.
- What you will wear.
- Who you will see.
- What will happen while you are there.

resolution   plane   then

car travel characters plot jacket climax

```
----------------------------------------
----------------------------------------
----------------------------------------
----------------------------------------
----------------------------------------
----------------------------------------
----------------------------------------
```

finally   hat   see   setting   conclusion   next   bike

Words That Are Nouns

A **noun** names a person, place, or thing.

Directions: Circle the two nouns in each sentence. The first one is done for you.

The pig has a curly tail. The hen is sitting on her nest.

A horse is in the barn. The goat has horns.

The cow has a calf. The farmer is painting the fence.

6

Words That Are Nouns

Directions: Use the words in the Word Bank to write the correct nouns in each box below.

Word Bank

girl	park	truck	vase
artist	tree	doctor	zoo
school	store	ball	baby

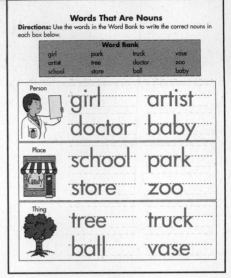

Person
girl   artist
doctor baby

Place
school park
store   zoo

Thing
tree   truck
ball   vase

7

Words That Are Nouns

Directions: Complete each sentence with the correct noun. Use the pictures to help you.

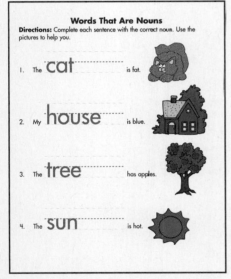

1. The **cat** is fat.

2. My **house** is blue.

3. The **tree** has apples.

4. The **sun** is hot.

8

Words About North America

North America is the third largest continent in the world. It has cold parts and hot parts. Rivers, mountains, lakes, plains, deserts, and canyons make up the land. Canada is the largest country in North America and reaches almost to the top of the world. The United States of America is the country in the middle. Mexico is the most southern country in North America.

Directions: Trace the words. Then, color the map of North America.

North America
United States of America
Mexico   Canada

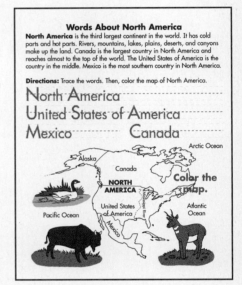

Color the map.

Arctic Ocean
Alaska   Canada
NORTH AMERICA
United States of America
Pacific Ocean   Mexico   Atlantic Ocean

9

Animal Words

Directions: Trace and write the animal names. Then, color the pictures.

Example:

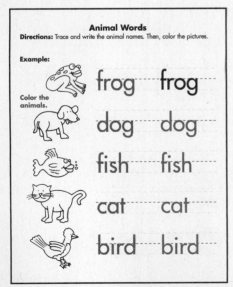

Color the animals.

frog frog
dog   dog
fish fish
cat   cat
bird bird

10

Animal Words

Directions: Write the missing letters for each word.

Example:

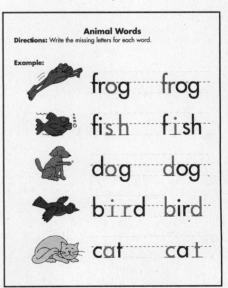

frog frog
fish fish
dog   dog
bird bird
cat   cat

11

Animal Words

Directions: These sentences tell about animals. Write the word that completes each sentence. Use the pictures to help you.

Example: My **frog** jumps high.

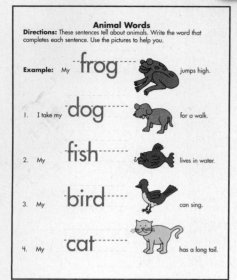

1. I take my **dog** for a walk.

2. My **fish** lives in water.

3. My **bird** can sing.

4. My **cat** has a long tail.

12

Number Words

Directions: Trace and write the number words. Then, color the numbers.

Example:

Color the numbers.

1	one	one
2	two	two
3	three	three
4	four	four
5	five	five
6	six	six
7	seven	seven
8	eight	eight
9	nine	nine
10	ten	ten

13

Words That Are Nouns

Directions: Use the words in the Word Bank to complete each sentence with the correct noun.

Word Bank
| ducks | sun | tree |
| dog | boys | bird |

1. A big **tree** grows in the park.

2. The **sun** is in the sky.

3. A **dog** digs a hole.

4. Three **ducks** swim in the water.

5. A **bird** sits on its nest.

6. Two **boys** fly a kite.

14

Words That Are Nouns

A **noun** names a person, place, or thing.

Directions: Circle the two nouns in each sentence.

1. The (boy) walks to (school.)

2. The (girl) carries a big (bag.)

3. The (teacher) writes on the (chalkboard.)

4. The (children) listen to (music.)

5. The (boy) plays with his (friend.)

6. The (girl) goes (home.)

15

Words That Are Nouns

Nouns tell the name of a person, place, or thing.

Directions: Look at each picture. Color it red if it names a person. Color it blue if it names a place. Color it green if it names a thing.

color blue — movie theater

color red — grandfather

color green — dinosaur

color green — flower

color blue — park

color red — girl

color green — grapes

color red — fireman

color blue — library

16

Words About the United States

President Jefferson chose Meriweather Lewis and William Clark to find a path to the Pacific Ocean. They had to draw maps of the land, record weather conditions, and write about the plants and animals they found along the way. People wanted to know what it was like west of the Mississippi River. On May 14, 1804, they started their journey. They arrived at the Pacific Ocean in the winter of 1805. They set up a camp that they named Fort Clatsop.

Directions: Write the names of the states in the order Lewis and Clark traveled through them.

1. Missouri
2. Kansas
3. Nebraska
4. Iowa
5. South Dakota
6. North Dakota
7. Montana
8. Idaho
9. Washington
10. Oregon

17

306

ANSWER key

Words About Birds

Birds are warm-blooded vertebrates (animals with backbones). They are unique animals because their bodies are covered with feathers. Instead of front legs or arms, birds have wings and most can fly.

Directions: Use the words in the Word Bank to answer each riddle. Then, label each bird part.

Word Bank
feathers   feet   bill   wings

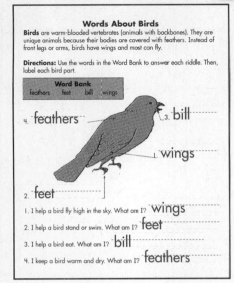

4. feathers — 3. bill

wings

2. feet

1. I help a bird fly high in the sky. What am I? **wings**

2. I help a bird stand or swim. What am I? **feet**

3. I help a bird eat. What am I? **bill**

4. I keep a bird warm and dry. What am I? **feathers**

18

Words About Birds

Directions: Use the words in the Word Bank to complete the puzzle about birds. Then, color only the birds.

Word Bank
feathers   bill   lungs   eggs   warm

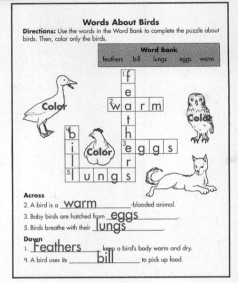

Across
2. A bird is a **warm** -blooded animal.
3. Baby birds are hatched from **eggs** .
5. Birds breathe with their **lungs** .

Down
1. **feathers** keep a bird's body warm and dry.
4. A bird uses its **bill** to pick up food.

19

Number Words

Directions: Count the items. Use the words in the Word Bank to complete the puzzles about number words.

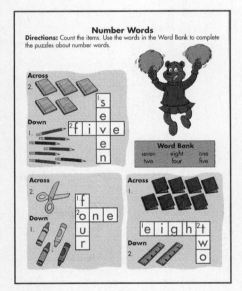

Across
2.

Down
1.   ²f i v e

Across
2.   ¹f
Down   ²o n e
1.   u
    r

Across
1.
¹e i g h ²t
Down   w
2.   o

Word Bank
seven   eight   one
two   four   five

21

Words That Are Nouns

Directions: The letters in each word are mixed up. Unscramble the letters and write each noun correctly. Use the Word Bank and the pictures to help you. Then, draw a line to match the words with the pictures.

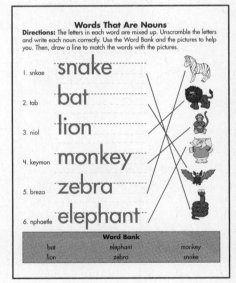

1. snkae   **snake**
2. tab   **bat**
3. niol   **lion**
4. keymon   **monkey**
5. breza   **zebra**
6. nphaetle   **elephant**

Word Bank
bat   elephant   monkey
lion   zebra   snake

22

Words That Are Nouns

Directions: Use the words in the Word Bank to write the correct noun in each box.

store   zoo   child   baby   teacher   table
cat   park   gym   woman   sock   horse

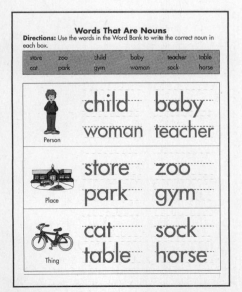

Person — **child   baby   woman   teacher**

Place — **store   zoo   park   gym**

Thing — **cat   sock   table   horse**

23

Words That Are Nouns

Directions: Circle the nouns in the Word Bank. Then, write the correct noun on each line.

Word Bank
teacher   up   dog   the   library
runs   is   cowboy   cap   zoo

dog   library   teacher

cap   cowboy   zoo

24

307

Words About South America

South America is the fourth largest continent. It stretches almost to the bottom of the world. The longest mountain range, the Andes, is located in South America. The largest tropical rainforest is there, too. The Amazon River runs across South America. It carries the most water of any river in the world.

Directions: Trace the words. Then, color the map of South America.

South America

mountain   river

rainforest

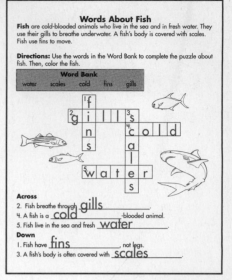

Pacific Ocean

Color the map.

Amazon River

SOUTH AMERICA

Andes Mountains

Atlantic Ocean

25

Words About Fish

Fish are cold-blooded animals who live in the sea and in fresh water. They use their gills to breathe underwater. A fish's body is covered with scales. Fish use fins to move.

Directions: Use the words in the Word Bank to complete the puzzle about fish. Then, color the fish.

Word Bank
water   scales   cold   fins   gills

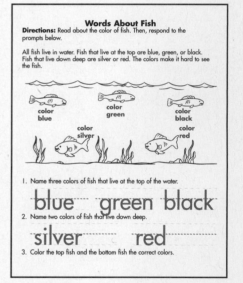

Puzzle:
¹f
²g i l l s   ³s
i   c⁴c o l d
n   a
s   l
⁵w a t e r   e
s

Across
2. Fish breathe through gills
4. A fish is a cold -blooded animal.
5. Fish live in the sea and fresh water

Down
1. Fish have fins , not legs.
3. A fish's body is often covered with scales

26

Words About Fish

Of all the animals with backbones, only fish and tadpoles have gills.

Directions: Use the words in the Word Bank to label each fish part.

Word Bank
gills   mouth   eye   nostril   fins   backbone

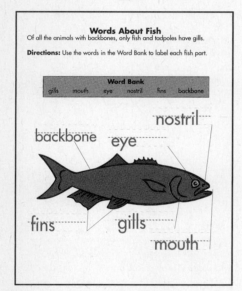

nostril

backbone   eye

fins   gills

mouth

27

Words About Fish

Directions: Read about the color of fish. Then, respond to the prompts below.

All fish live in water. Fish that live at the top are blue, green, or black. Fish that live down deep are silver or red. The colors make it hard to see the fish.

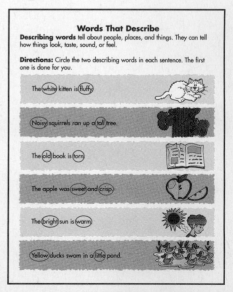

color blue   color green   color black

color silver   color red

1. Name three colors of fish that live at the top of the water.

blue   green   black

2. Name two colors of fish that live down deep.

silver   red

3. Color the top fish and the bottom fish the correct colors.

28

Unit I Review

Directions: Fill in the correct number word that answers each question.

1. How many countries make up North America? three

2. How many number words from 1 to 10 have only three letters? four

3. How many states did Lewis and Clark travel through to reach the Pacific Ocean? ten

Directions: Circle the nouns in each sentence.

1. The (dog) buries its (bone)
2. The (boys) play in the (park)
3. A (bird) has (feathers) to keep it warm.
4. A (monkey) swings on a (branch)
5. A (fish) lives in (water)
6. The (teacher) likes her (students)

29

Words That Describe

Describing words tell about people, places, and things. They can tell how things look, taste, sound, or feel.

Directions: Circle the two describing words in each sentence. The first one is done for you.

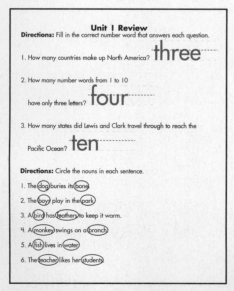

The (white) kitten is (fluffy)

(Noisy) squirrels ran up a (tall) tree.

The (old) book is (torn)

The apple was (sweet) and (crisp)

The (bright) sun is (warm)

(Yellow) ducks swam in a (little) pond.

31

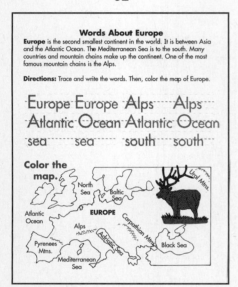

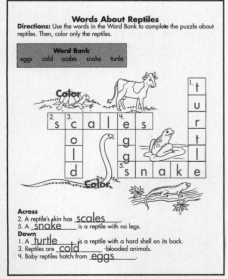

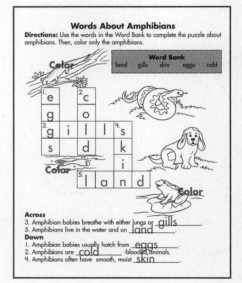

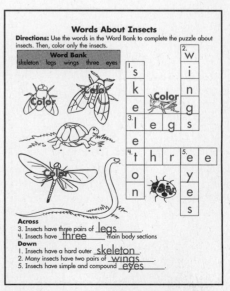

Words That Describe

Some words describe a person, place, or thing. These words tell more about a naming word.

Example: The shoe is **old**.

Directions: Use the words in the Word Bank to write the correct describing word in each box.

cold   round   funny   light   sad   fat

cold

light

funny

fat

sad

round

32

Words That Describe

A **describing word** tells about a noun. It can tell what kind, what color, what size, what shape, or how many.

Directions: Use the words in the Word Bank to complete each sentence with the correct describing word.

green   big   three   round   bushy   six

1. A _____ has **big** teeth.
2. A _____ has a **bushy** tail.
3. A _____ has **six** legs.
4. The _____ will become a **green** frog.
5. The **three** _____ hang by their tails.
6. An _____ has **round** eyes.

33

Words About Europe

Europe is the second smallest continent in the world. It is between Asia and the Atlantic Ocean. The Mediterranean Sea is to the south. Many countries and mountain chains make up the continent. One of the most famous mountain chains is the Alps.

Directions: Trace and write the words. Then, color the map of Europe.

Europe   Europe   Alps   Alps
Atlantic Ocean   Atlantic Ocean
sea   sea   south   south

Color the map.

North Sea   Baltic Sea   Ural Mtns.
Atlantic Ocean   EUROPE   Carpathian Mtns.
Alps   Adriatic Sea
Pyrenees Mtns.   Black Sea
Mediterranean Sea

34

Words About Amphibians

Directions: Use the words in the Word Bank to complete the puzzle about amphibians. Then, color only the amphibians.

Color

Word Bank
land   gills   skin   eggs   cold

Color

Color

Across
3. Amphibian babies breathe with either lungs or **gills**
5. Amphibians live in the water and on **land**
Down
1. Amphibian babies usually hatch from **eggs**
2. Amphibians are **cold** -blooded animals.
4. Amphibians often have smooth, moist **skin**

35

Words About Reptiles

Directions: Use the words in the Word Bank to complete the puzzle about reptiles. Then, color only the reptiles.

Word Bank
eggs   cold   scales   snake   turtle

Color

Color

Across
2. A reptile's skin has **scales**
5. A **snake** is a reptile with no legs.
Down
1. A **turtle** is a reptile with a hard shell on its back.
3. Reptiles are **cold** -blooded animals.
4. Baby reptiles hatch from **eggs**

36

309

Words About Insects

Directions: Use the words in the Word Bank to complete the puzzle about insects. Then, color only the insects.

Word Bank
skeleton   legs   wings   three   eyes

Color

Color

Color

Across
3. Insects have three pairs of **legs**
4. Insects have **three** main body sections.
Down
1. Insects have a hard outer **skeleton**
2. Many insects have two pairs of **wings**
5. Insects have simple and compound **eyes**

37

Spanish Number Words

1	one	uno	(ōō-nō)
2	two	dos	(dōs)
3	three	tres	(trās)
4	four	cuatro	(kwŏ-trō)
5	five	cinco	(sēn-ko)
6	six	seis	(sās)
7	seven	siete	(sē-ē-tā)
8	eight	ocho	(ō-chō)
9	nine	nueve	(nōō-ā-vā)
10	ten	diez	(dē-ēz)

Directions: Read each number word. Say each number word in Spanish. Then, write the Spanish word next to the English word.

one **uno**　four **cuatro**

seven **siete**　three **tres**

nine **nueve**　eight **ocho**

ten **diez**　six **seis**

two **dos**　five **cinco**

38

Words That Describe

Directions: Circle the describing word in each sentence. Draw a line from each sentence to the picture it describes.

1. The (hungry) dog is eating.
2. The (tiny) bird is flying.
3. Horses have (long) legs.
4. She is a (fast) runner.
5. The (little) boy was lost.

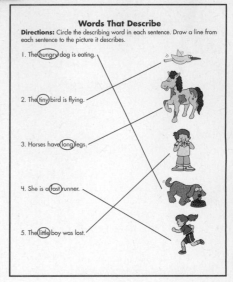

39

Words That Describe

Directions: Draw a line from each word to the picture it describes.

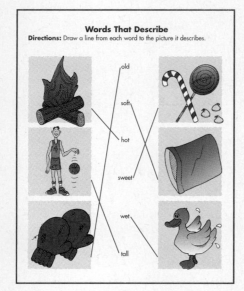

old, soft, hot, sweet, wet, tall

40

Words That Describe

Directions: Use the words in the Word Bank to write the correct describing word in each box.

Word Bank: wet　round　funny　soft　sad　tall

soft　tall

funny　sad

round　wet

41

Words About Antarctica

Antarctica, the fifth largest continent, is the most southern continent. It is covered with ice and is so cold in the winter that only scientists and exploration groups live there. No animals live on the ice, but many live along the edge of the ice by the sea.

Directions: Trace and write the words. Then, color the map of Antarctica.

Antarctica　Antarctica
ice　ice　cold　cold
scientist　scientist

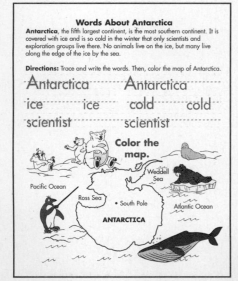

Color the map.

42

310

Words About Mammals

Directions: Use the words in the Word Bank to complete the puzzle about mammals. Then, color only the mammals.

Word Bank: hair　babies　lungs　milk　warm

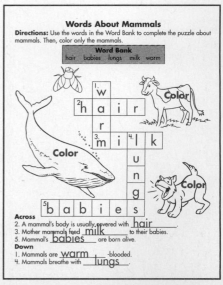

Across
2. A mammal's body is usually covered with **hair**.
3. Mother mammals feed **milk** to their babies.
5. Mammal's **babies** are born alive.
Down
1. Mammals are **warm**-blooded.
4. Mammals breathe with **lungs**.

43

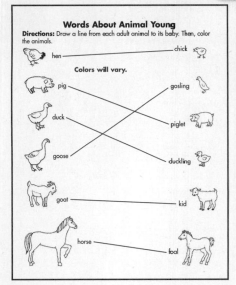

Words About Animal Young
Directions: Draw a line from each adult animal to its baby. Then, color the animals.

hen —————— chick

Colors will vary.

pig —————— gosling
duck —————— piglet
goose —————— duckling
goat —————— kid
horse —————— foal

44

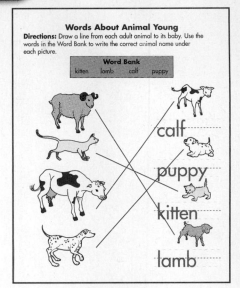

Words About Animal Young
Directions: Draw a line from each adult animal to its baby. Use the words in the Word Bank to write the correct animal name under each picture.

Word Bank
kitten lamb calf puppy

calf
puppy
kitten
lamb

45

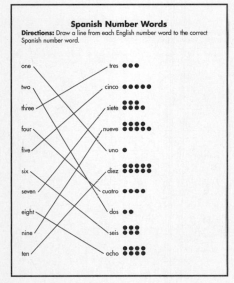

Spanish Number Words
Directions: Draw a line from each English number word to the correct Spanish number word.

one — tres •••
two — cinco •••••
three — siete ••••
four — nueve ••••
five — uno •
six — diez •••••
seven — cuatro ••••
eight — dos ••
nine — seis •••
ten — ocho ••••

46

Words That Are Adjectives
Describing words are also called **adjectives**.

Directions: Circle the describing word in each sentence.

1. The (juicy) apple is on the plate.
2. The (furry) dog is eating the bone.
3. It was a (sunny) day.
4. The kitten drinks (warm) milk.
5. The baby has a (loud) cry.

47

Words That Are Adjectives
Directions: Draw a picture of your favorite animal. Write two sentences that tell about your picture. Make sure to use a describing word in each sentence.

Pictures will vary.

Sentences will vary.

48

Words That Are Adjectives
Adjectives tell us more about a person, place, or thing.

Directions: Use the words in the Word Bank to write the correct adjective next to each picture.

Word Bank
happy round sick cold long

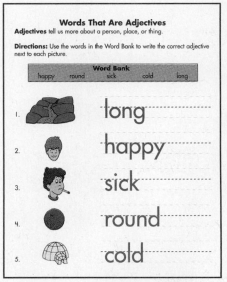

1. long
2. happy
3. sick
4. round
5. cold

49

Words About Australia

Australia is the smallest continent in the world. It is an island in the South Pacific Ocean. Much of Australia is desert, so there are not many people who live there. Since Australia is so far away from the other continents, its animals look very different.

Directions: Trace the words. Then, color the map of Australia.

Australia   continent

Pacific Ocean

island   desert

Color the map.

Choral Sea

Indian Ocean

AUSTRALIA

Pacific Ocean

Indian Ocean   Tasman Sea

50

Words About Zoo Animals

Directions: Write the name of the animal that answers each riddle. Use the pictures and animal words to help you.

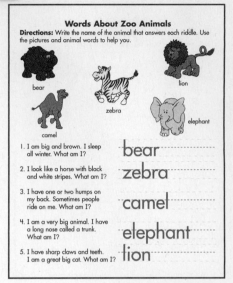

bear   lion

zebra

camel   elephant

1. I am big and brown. I sleep all winter. What am I?

2. I look like a horse with black and white stripes. What am I?

3. I have one or two humps on my back. Sometimes people ride on me. What am I?

4. I am a very big animal. I have a long nose called a trunk. What am I?

5. I have sharp claws and teeth. I am a great big cat. What am I?

bear

zebra

camel

elephant

lion

51

Words About Farm Animals

Directions: Read the story. Then, answer the questions.

You can hear many sounds on the farm. Roosters crow in the morning. The cows moo, and the donkeys say, "hee-haw." You might even hear the tractor motor humming.

1. What animal crows in the morning?   rooster

2. What sound does the cow make?   moo

3. What in the story is not an animal?   tractor

4. What animals say, "hee-haw"?   donkey

Directions: Use the words in the Word Bank to find the farm words. Look up, down, and across.

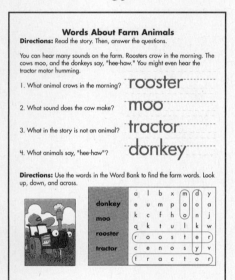

donkey

moo

rooster

tractor

a	l	b	x	m	d	y
e	u	m	p	o	o	a
k	c	f	h	o	o	j
q	k	t	u	l	k	w
r	o	o	s	t	e	r
c	e	n	o	s	y	v
t	r	a	c	t	o	r

52

Words About Zoo and Farm Animals

Directions: Read the story. Then, use the words in the Word Bank to complete the puzzle about zoo and farm animals.

The zoo is for wild animals. Tigers live at the zoo. Some snakes live at the zoo. The farm is for tame animals. Ducks and donkeys live on farms.

Word Bank

ducks   snakes

tigers   donkeys

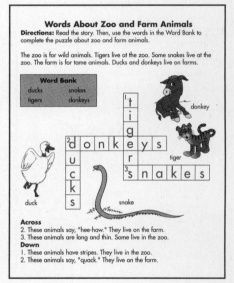

donkey

tiger

duck   snake

Across
2. These animals say, "hee-haw." They live on the farm.
3. These animals are long and thin. Some live in the zoo.
Down
1. These animals have stripes. They live in the zoo.
2. These animals say, "quack." They live on the farm.

53

Unit 2 Review

Directions: Circle the describing words in each sentence.

1. Amphibians have (smooth) skin.

2. A turtle has a (hard) shell on its back.

3. The (little) puppy will grow into a (big) dog.

4. Antarctica is a (cold) continent.

5. (Wild) animals live at the zoo.

Directions: Trace the words. Then, write the correct word to answer each question.

yes   no

1. Is Australia an island in the Atlantic Ocean?   no

2. Do mammals breathe with lungs?   yes

3. Does a zebra have black and white stripes?   yes

4. Is siete the Spanish word for six?   no

5. Does a cow say, "hee-haw"?   no

54

Action Words

An **action word** tells what a person or thing can do.

Example: Fred **kicks** the ball.

Directions: Circle the action word that tells what each child is doing.

(jump)   (sleep)
boy   bed

hello   (skate)
(talk)   mittens

(hop)
sidewalk   (sing)
        song

(swim)   story
deep   (read)

56

Action Words

Action words tell things we can do.

Directions: Trace and write the action words. The first one is done for you.

1. sleep sleep
2. run run
3. make make
4. ride ride
5. play play
6. stop stop

57

Action Words

Directions: Underline the action word in each sentence. Then, draw a line from each sentence to the picture it describes. The first one is done for you.

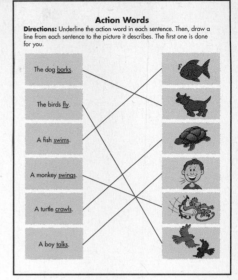

The dog <u>barks</u>.

The birds <u>fly</u>.

A fish <u>swims</u>.

A monkey <u>swings</u>.

A turtle <u>crawls</u>.

A boy <u>talks</u>.

58

Words About Africa

Africa is the second largest continent in the world. Almost all of Africa is a hot, dry desert. It is the largest desert in the world. The desert is called the Sahara. The longest river in the world, the Nile River, flows through Africa. Many big animals live in the forests of central Africa where it is hot, but plants and trees grow well because there are heavy rains.

Directions: Trace and write the words. Then, color the map of Africa.

Africa Africa desert desert
rain rain river river

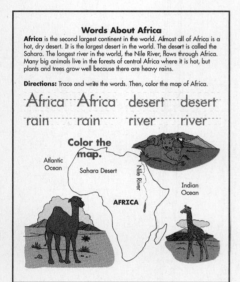

Color the map.

Atlantic Ocean
Sahara Desert
Nile River
AFRICA
Indian Ocean

59

Weather Words

Directions: Trace and write the weather words. Then, color the pictures. The first one is done for you.

Color the pictures.

sun sun
snow snow
hot hot
rain rain
wet wet
cold cold

60

Weather Words

Directions: The letters in each weather word are mixed up. Unscramble the letters and write each word correctly. The first one is done for you.

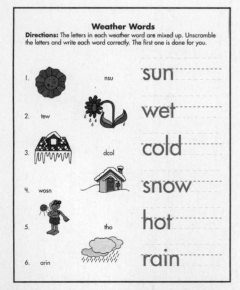

1. nsu sun
2. tew wet
3. dcol cold
4. wosn snow
5. tho hot
6. arin rain

61

Weather Words

Directions: Use the words in the Word Bank to complete each sentence with the correct weather word. Put a period at the end of the telling sentences and a question mark at the end of the asking sentences. The first one is done for you.

Word Bank
rain   water   wet   hot

1. The sun makes me hot .
2. When it rains, the grass gets wet .
3. Do you think it will rain on our picnic ?
4. Should you drink the water from the rain ?

62

ANSWER key

Number Words

Directions: Draw a line from each number to the correct number word.

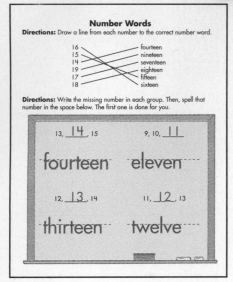

16 — fourteen
15 — nineteen
14 — seventeen
19 — eighteen
17 — fifteen
18 — sixteen

Directions: Write the missing number in each group. Then, spell that number in the space below. The first one is done for you.

13, __14__, 15   9, 10, __11__

fourteen   **eleven**

12, __13__, 14   11, __12__, 13

thirteen   **twelve**

63

Words That Are Verbs

A **verb** is an action word. A verb tells what a person or thing does.

Example: Jane **reads** a book.

Directions: Circle the verb in each sentence.

Two tiny dogs (dance)

The bear (climbs) a ladder.

The clown (falls) down.

A tiger (jumps) through a ring.

A boy (eats) popcorn.

A woman (swings) on a trapeze.

64

Words That Are Verbs

Directions: Use the words in the Word Bank to complete each sentence with the correct verb.

Word Bank
play   jump   stop   ride   make   run

One day, Mom said I could **ride** the school bus home with Pat. We watched Pat's **play** with a ⬤. Then, Pat told me, "My mother said she would **make** some 🍪 . I'll get us some."

Pat went inside to get the 🍪 . Just then, I saw a **run** into the yard. Oh, no! He might chase Pat's 🐱 . I had to **stop** him!

Pat came back with the 🍪 . The 🐶 began to **jump** on Pat and lick Pat's face. Then, he ran off with the 🍪 .

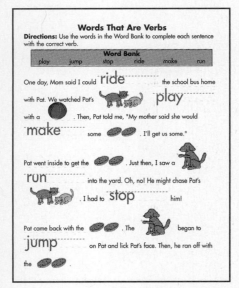

65

Words That Are Verbs

Directions: Use the words in the Word Bank to write five sentences. Use a different verb for each sentence.

Word Bank
catch   color   eat   grow   fly

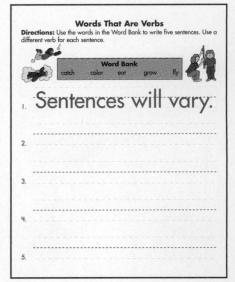

1. **Sentences will vary.**

2. _____

3. _____

4. _____

5. _____

66

Words About Asia

Asia is the world's largest continent. More than one-half of all the people in the world live in Asia. Asia contains Russia, which is the largest country in the world. China, the country that is home to the most people in the world, is also in Asia. The tallest mountains in the world are in India, a country that is in Asia.

Directions: Trace and write the words. Then, color the map of Asia.

Asia   Asia   Russia   Russia
China   China   India   India

Color the map.

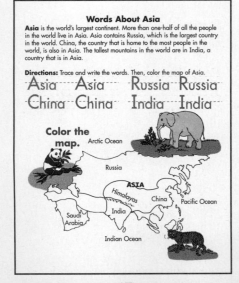

Arctic Ocean
Russia
ASIA
Himalayas   China
Saudi Arabia   India   Pacific Ocean
Indian Ocean

67

Winter Words

Directions: Read about winter. Look at the picture. Then, complete the activities. There may be more than one correct answer.

Winter can be cold and snowy. Animals stay near each other to stay warm. People wear coats, hats, and gloves. Children make snowmen. It is fun to play in the snow.

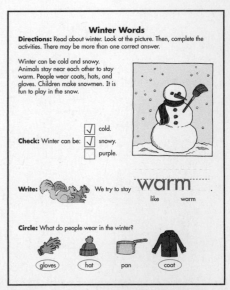

Check: Winter can be:
☑ cold.
☑ snowy.
☐ purple.

Write: We try to stay **warm**
like   warm

Circle: What do people wear in the winter?

(gloves)   (hat)   pan   (coat)

68

314

Spring Words

Directions: Read about spring. Look at the picture. Then, complete the activities. There may be more than one correct answer.

It is warm in the spring. Flowers begin to bloom. Trees have new leaves. Birds make their nests and lay eggs.

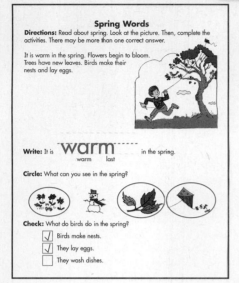

Write: It is **warm** in the spring.
warm   last

Circle: What can you see in the spring?

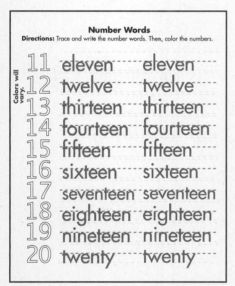

Check: What do birds do in the spring?
- ☑ Birds make nests.
- ☑ They lay eggs.
- ☐ They wash dishes.

69

Summer Words

Directions: Read about summer. Look at the picture. Then, complete the activities. There may be more than one correct answer.

Summer can be very hot. It is the time when children are out of school. They have fun playing with friends, swimming to stay cool, and sometimes going on family picnics and vacations.

Write: Summer can be very **hot**
purple   hot

Check: What happens in the summer?
- ☑ Children are out of school.
- ☐ Skunks go on picnics.
- ☑ Children play with friends.

Write: What do you like to do in the summer?

Answers will vary.

70

Number Words

Directions: Trace and write the number words. Then, color the numbers.

Colors will vary.

11	eleven	eleven
12	twelve	twelve
13	thirteen	thirteen
14	fourteen	fourteen
15	fifteen	fifteen
16	sixteen	sixteen
17	seventeen	seventeen
18	eighteen	eighteen
19	nineteen	nineteen
20	twenty	twenty

71

Words That Are Verbs

The words **is**, **are**, and **am** are special verbs.

Use **is** to tell about one person or thing.
Use **are** to tell about more than one thing.
Use **are** with the word you.
Use **am** with the word I.

Directions: Write **is**, **are**, or **am** to complete each sentence.

1. The lake **is** deep.

2. Many fish **are** under the water.

3. I **am** at the lake.

4. Sally **is** with me.

5. We **are** busy catching fish.

6. You **are** welcome to join us.

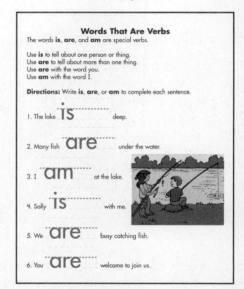

72

Words That Are Verbs

Use **is** in sentences about one person or one thing. Use **are** in sentences about more than one person or thing.

Example: The dog **is** barking.
The dogs **are** barking.

Directions: Write **is** or **are** to complete each sentence.

1. Jim **is** playing baseball.

2. Fred and Sam **are** good friends.

3. Cupcakes **are** my favorite treat.

4. Lisa **is** a good soccer player.

73

Words That Are Verbs

Directions: Write **is** or **are** to complete each sentence.

1. Cats and dogs **are** good pets.

2. Bill **is** my best friend.

3. Apples **are** good to eat.

4. Pedro **is** coming to my house.

5. We **are** going to the zoo.

6. When **are** you all going to the zoo?

74

Words About the Continents

Directions: The letters in each word are mixed up. Unscramble the letters and write the name of each continent correctly. Use the Word Bank to help you.

Word Bank		
Africa	Australia	North America	Antarctica
Asia	Europe	South America	

1. rtonh miecara North America
2. cfiara Africa
3. eropeu Europe
4. uhots ecaamir South America
5. saia Asia
6. tnrtaiacac Antarctica
7. asurilaat Australia

75

Autumn Words

Directions: Read about autumn. Look at the picture. Then, complete the activities. There may be more than one correct answer.

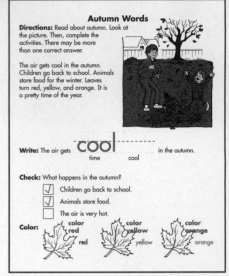

The air gets cool in the autumn. Children go back to school. Animals store food for the winter. Leaves turn red, yellow, and orange. It is a pretty time of the year.

Write: The air gets cool in the autumn.
time cool

Check: What happens in the autumn?
☑ Children go back to school.
☑ Animals store food.
☐ The air is very hot.

Color: color red color yellow color orange
red yellow orange

76

Autumn Words

Directions: Read about raking leaves. Then, answer the questions.

I like to rake leaves. Do you? Leaves die each year. They get brown and dry. They fall from the trees. Then, people rake them up.

1. What color are leaves when they die?

Leaves are brown when they die.

2. What happens when they die?

They fall from the trees.

3. What do people do when leaves fall?

People rake the leaves.

77

Words About Seasons

Directions:
1. Use the words in the Word Bank to write the correct season under each picture.
2. Color the clothes for autumn blue.
3. Color the clothes for winter red.
4. Color the clothes for spring green.
5. Color the clothes for summer yellow.

Word Bank	
Spring	Summer
Autumn	Winter

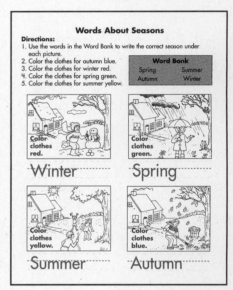

Color clothes red. Winter
Color clothes green. Spring
Color clothes yellow. Summer
Color clothes blue. Autumn

78

Unit 3 Review

Directions: Use the words in the Word Bank to complete each sentence.

Word Bank						
snow	are	China	desert	flows	jump	fly	sixteen

1. I like to jump in the autumn leaves.
2. The number sixteen comes after fifteen.
3. The Sahara is the largest desert in the world.
4. The Nile River flows through Africa.
5. There are seven continents in the world.
6. Our town gets a lot of snow in the winter.
7. Russia, China , and India are all part of Asia.
8. My family will fly to Australia for our summer vacation.

79

Words That Are Pronouns

Sometimes we use other words to name people. For a boy or a man, we use **he**. For a girl or a woman, we use **she**. For two or more people, we use **they**. He, she, and they are called **pronouns**.

Directions: Write **he, she,** or **they** to complete each sentence. The first one is done for you.

1. The boy likes cookies.

He likes cookies.

2. The girl is running fast.

She is running fast.

3. The woman has a cold.

She has a cold.

4. Two children came to school.

They came to school.

81

Words That Are Pronouns

Pronouns are words that you can use instead of nouns. **She**, **he**, **it**, and **they** are pronouns.

Directions: Read each sentence. Then, complete each sentence with the correct pronoun.

1. Dan likes funny jokes.   **He** likes funny jokes.

2. Peg and Sam went to the zoo.   **They** went to the zoo.

3. The dog digs in the yard.   **It** likes to dig in the yard.

4. Sara is a very good dancer.   **She** is a very good dancer.

5. Fred and Ed are twins.   **They** are twins.

82

Words That Are Pronouns

A **pronoun** is a word that can take the place of a noun in a sentence.

Example:
My dad is a pilot. **He** flies airplanes.

Directions: Circle the pronoun that can take the place of the bold words in each sentence.

1. **My mother** is a pilot, too.   They   (She)

2. **Mom and Dad** own a small plane.   We   (They)

3. **My brother** wants to be a pilot.   It   (He)

4. **Mother** says flying is fun.   (She)   He

5. **Dad** loves to fly.   They   (He)

6. **My brother** is older than I am.   (He)   We

83

Community Words

Directions: Look at the map. Use the words in the Word Bank to write the correct name under each place. Then, color the map.

Word Bank					
school	city	home	lake	pond	store

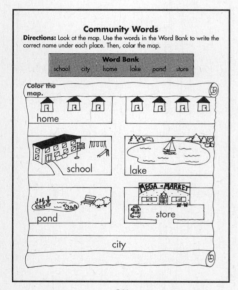

Color the map.

home

school   lake

pond   store

city

84

Time of Day Words

Directions: Trace and write the time of day words. Then, look at each picture. Write **day** or **night** on each line to tell the time.

day   day   day

night   night   night

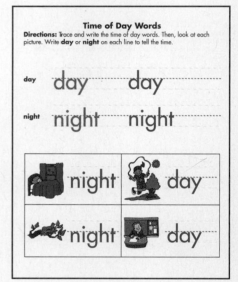

night   day

night   day

85

Time of Day Words

Directions: Use the words in the Word Bank to write the correct time of day words under each picture.

Word Bank							
stars	sun	moon	rays	dark	light	night	day

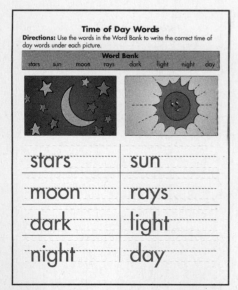

stars	sun
moon	rays
dark	light
night	day

86

Space Words

Directions: Read about the night sky. Look at the picture. Then, complete the activities.

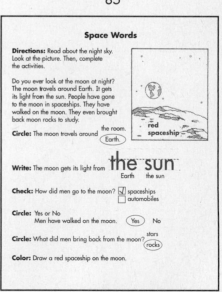

Do you ever look at the moon at night? The moon travels around Earth. It gets its light from the sun. People have gone to the moon in spaceships. They have walked on the moon. They even brought back moon rocks to study.

Circle: The moon travels around   the room.   (Earth.)

red spaceship

Write: The moon gets its light from   **the sun**
Earth   the sun

Check: How did men go to the moon?   ☑ spaceships   ☐ automobiles

Circle: Yes or No
Men have walked on the moon.   (Yes)   No

Circle: What did men bring back from the moon?   stars   (rocks)

Color: Draw a red spaceship on the moon.

87

Ordinal Number Words

Directions: Use the words in the Word Bank to write the correct ordinal number word on each line.

Word Bank				
second	fifth	seventh	first	tenth
third	eighth	sixth	fourth	ninth

1. first
2. second
3. third
4. fourth
5. fifth
6. sixth
7. seventh
8. eighth
9. ninth
10. tenth

Directions: Underline the word that tells which picture is circled in each row.

1. ● ● ● ● ● ⊙ ● ● ● ●   fourth   <u>sixth</u>
2. 🌐 🌐 ⊙ 🌐 🌐 🌐 🌐 🌐 🌐 🌐   <u>third</u>   fifth

88

Words That Are Articles

Articles are small words that help us better understand nouns. **A** and **an** are articles. Use **a** before a word that begins with a consonant. Use **an** before a word that begins with a vowel.

Example: We looked in **a** nest. It had **an** eagle in it.

Directions: Write **a** or **an** to complete each sentence. The first one is done for you.

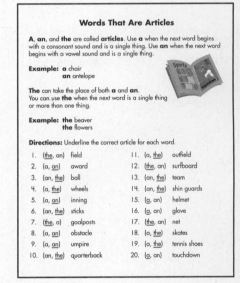

I found **a** book. It had a story about **an** ant in it. In the story, **a** lion gave three wishes to **an** ant. The ant's first wish was to ride **an** elephant. The second wish was to ride **an** alligator. The last wish was **a** wish for three more wishes.

89

Words That Are Articles

Articles are words that come before nouns. **A** and **an** are articles. Use **a** before a word that begins with a consonant. Use **an** before a word that begins with a vowel.

Example: **a** peach   **an** apple

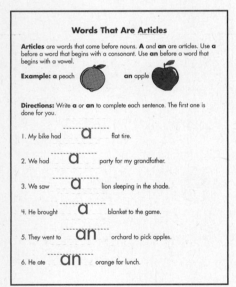

Directions: Write **a** or **an** to complete each sentence. The first one is done for you.

1. My bike had **a** flat tire.
2. We had **a** party for my grandfather.
3. We saw **a** lion sleeping in the shade.
4. He brought **a** blanket to the game.
5. They went to **an** orchard to pick apples.
6. He ate **an** orange for lunch.

90

Words That Are Articles

A, **an**, and **the** are called **articles**. Use **a** when the next word begins with a consonant sound and is a single thing. Use **an** when the next word begins with a vowel sound and is a single thing.

Example: **a** chair
an antelope

The can take the place of both **a** and **an**. You can use **the** when the next word is a single thing or more than one thing.

Example: **the** beaver
the flowers

Directions: Underline the correct article for each word.

1. (<u>the</u>, an) field
2. (a, <u>an</u>) award
3. (an, <u>the</u>) ball
4. (a, <u>the</u>) wheels
5. (a, <u>an</u>) inning
6. (an, <u>the</u>) sticks
7. (<u>the</u>, a) goalposts
8. (a, <u>an</u>) obstacle
9. (a, <u>an</u>) umpire
10. (an, <u>the</u>) quarterback
11. (a, <u>the</u>) outfield
12. (<u>the</u>, an) surfboard
13. (an, <u>the</u>) team
14. (an, <u>the</u>) shin guards
15. (<u>a</u>, an) helmet
16. (<u>a</u>, an) glove
17. (<u>the</u>, an) net
18. (a, <u>the</u>) skates
19. (a, <u>the</u>) tennis shoes
20. (<u>a</u>, an) touchdown

91

Community Words

Directions: Use the words in the Word Bank to write the correct community word in each sentence.

Word Bank			
hospital	bookstore	bakery	park

1. My mom loves doughnuts. Dad and I wanted to surprise her with some. We stopped at the

bakery

2. I love to read books! My mom said she would buy me a book at the

bookstore

3. I hurt my ankle at my basketball game. My coach took me to the

hospital

4. It was a warm summer day, and my family went to the

park

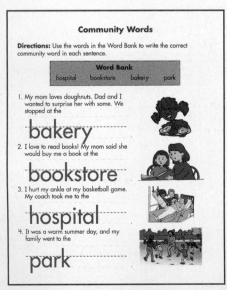

92

Space Words

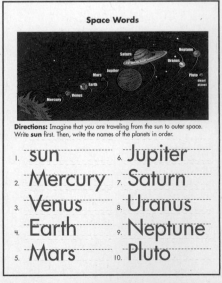

Directions: Imagine that you are traveling from the sun to outer space. Write **sun** first. Then, write the names of the planets in order.

1. sun
2. Mercury
3. Venus
4. Earth
5. Mars
6. Jupiter
7. Saturn
8. Uranus
9. Neptune
10. Pluto

93

Space Words

Directions: Read about Earth. Look at the picture. Then, complete the activities. There may be more than one correct answer.

yellow moon

• Colors may vary.

Earth is a planet. It is the planet where we live. Earth has land and water. It gets light and heat from the sun. Earth has one moon. Many people think there is life on other planets. Earth is the only planet that we know has life.

Unscramble: Earth is the **planet** where we live.
l e t p n a

Check:

- ☑ I have land and water.
- ☑ I get light and heat from the sun.
- ☐ I have five moons.
- ☑ I have one moon.
- ☑ I am a planet.

Circle: Earth is the only planet that we know has ~~stars.~~ (life.)

Color: Color the picture of Earth. Draw one yellow moon in the picture.

94

Space Words

Directions: Use the words in the Word Bank to answer each riddle.

Word Bank
float
stars
Mars
sun
Earth
craters
shuttle
Saturn

1. This huge star lights the day. **sun**
2. These shine at night. **stars**
3. These are on the moon. **craters**
4. This is our home planet. **Earth**
5. This flies into space. **shuttle**
6. This planet is red. **Mars**
7. This planet has rings. **Saturn**
8. Astronauts do this in space. **float**

95

Ordinal Number Words

Ordinal numbers show order in a series of things. **First**, **second**, and **third** are ordinal numbers.

Directions: Draw a line from each ordinal number to the correct picture.

eighth — 1st
second — 7th
third — 10th
fourth — 2nd
first — 4th
sixth — 6th
fifth — 8th
ninth — 9th
seventh — 3rd
tenth — 5th

96

Words With Prefixes

A **prefix** is a word part that you can add to the beginning of a word to change its meaning.

Directions: Read each prefix and its meaning. Add the prefix to the root word to make a new word. Then, complete each sentence with the correct word.

Prefixes	(Meaning)	Root Word	New Word
bi	(two)	cycle	bicycle
dis	(away from)	appear	disappear
mis	(wrong)	place	misplace
pre	(before)	school	preschool

1. Did you go to **preschool** before kindergarten?
2. The magician made the rabbit **disappear**
3. Put your things where they belong so you don't **misplace** them.
4. Can you ride a **bicycle** ?

97

Words With Suffixes

A **suffix** is a word part that you can add to the end of a word to change its meaning.

Directions: Read each suffix and its meaning.
The suffix **ful** means "full of." **Cheerful** means "full of cheer."
The suffix **less** means "without." **Cloudless** means "without clouds."
The suffix **ness** means "a state of being." **Darkness** means "being dark."
The suffix **ly** means "in this way." **Slowly** means "in a slow way."

Directions: Add the suffixes to the words to make new words.

1. care + ful = **careful**
2. pain + less = **painless**
3. brave + ly = **bravely**
4. sad + ly = **sadly**
5. sick + ness = **sickness**

98

Words With Prefixes and Suffixes

Directions: See how many new words you can make by adding prefixes and suffixes to the root words. You can use the prefixes, suffixes, and root words as many times as you like.

Prefixes:
bi   dis   ex   mis   pre

Root Words:
play   obey   friend   feel   health
polite   kind   thought   cycle   like

Suffixes:
ly   ful   ness   less

Suggested answers:

1. **bicycle**
2. **disobey**
3. **dislike**
4. **playful**
5. **politely**
6. **politeness**
7. **friendly**
8. **thoughtful**
9. **healthful**
10. **likely**
11. **kindly**
12. **kindness**

99

ANSWER key

Community Words

Directions: Trace the word. Then, complete each sentence with the word. Draw a picture of a house.

house **house**

Here is my **house** . I like my **house** .

Pictures will vary.

100

Sky, Land, and Sea Words

Directions: Read the words in the Word Bank.
Draw a circle around the sky words.
Draw a line under the land words.
Draw a box around the sea words.
Then, write the correct sky, land, and sea words in each box.

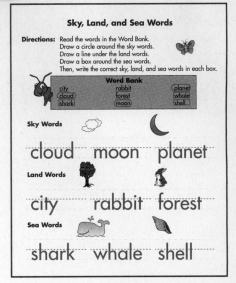

Word Bank

city	rabbit	planet
cloud	forest	whale
shark	moon	shell

Sky Words

cloud   moon   planet

Land Words

city   rabbit   forest

Sea Words

shark   whale   shell

101

Words for Living and Nonliving Things

Directions: Read about living and nonliving things. Then, answer the questions.

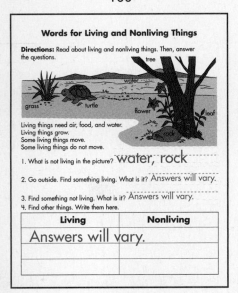

tree
water
grass   turtle   flower   leaf
rock

Living things need air, food, and water.
Living things grow.
Some living things move.
Some living things do not move.

1. What is not living in the picture? **water, rock**

2. Go outside. Find something living. What is it? Answers will vary.

3. Find something not living. What is it? Answers will vary.
4. Find other things. Write them here.

Living	Nonliving
Answers will vary.	

102

Words for Living and Nonliving Things

Directions: Use the words on the treasure chest to write the correct things in each list.

Living	Nonliving
1. girl	1. car
2. hen	2. house
3. dog	3. boat
4. bird	4. plane
5. tree	5. window
6. cow	6. rock

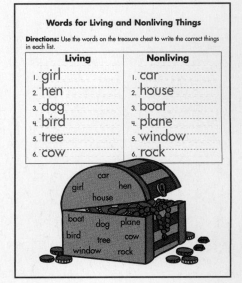

car
girl   hen
house
boat   dog   plane
bird   tree   cow
window   rock

103

Unit 4 Review

Directions: Draw a line to match each word or words to the correct description.

1. night
2. sickness
3. he, she, they
4. house
5. third
6. sun
7. a, an, the
8. spaceship
9. school
10. bicycle
11. whale
12. living things

Children go here to learn.
People use this to go to the moon.
This shines during the day.
This belongs in the sea.
These are pronouns.
This word has the prefix "bi."
This means "being sick."
Earth is in this position from the sun.
This is when you go to bed.
These are articles.
These need air, food, and water.
Some people live in this.

104

Words That Are Prepositions

Prepositions are words that show a connection between a noun or pronoun and another word. **Over** and **under** are prepositions.

Directions: Trace and write the preposition words. Then, circle the word that completes each sentence. Write it on the line.

over **over**   **over**

under **under**   **under**

1. The kite is **under** the tree.   over (under)

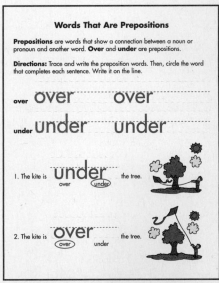

2. The kite is **over** the tree.   (over) under

106

320

Words That Are Prepositions

Prepositions are words that show a connection between a noun or pronoun and another word. **Above** and **below** are prepositions.

Directions: Trace and write the preposition words. Then, circle the word that completes each sentence. Write it on the line.

above **above   above**

below **below   below**

1. The fish is **below** the water.
   above (below)

2. The fish is **above** the water.
   (above) below

107

Words That Are Prepositions

A **preposition** is a word that shows a connection between a noun or pronoun and another word. **Inside** and **outside** are prepositions.

Directions: Trace and write the preposition words. Then, circle the word that completes each sentence. Write it on the line.

inside **inside   inside**

outside **outside   outside**

1. The dog is **inside** his house.
   (inside) outside

2. The dog is **outside** his house.
   inside (outside)

108

Words About Historical Figures

Martin Luther King, Jr. was an important black leader of the civil rights movement. Martin Luther King Day is a holiday we celebrate in January to honor his birthday.

Directions: Trace the words.

Martin Luther King, Jr.
civil rights
holiday

Directions: Martin Luther King, Jr.'s birthday is January 15. The holiday we use to honor him is celebrated each year on the third Monday of January. On the calendar below, color Martin Luther King, Jr.'s birthday red. Then, color the day it is celebrated blue.

109

Words About Nature

Directions: Trace and write the nature words. The first one is done for you.

 tree   tree

 grass   grass

flower   flower

pond   pond

sand   sand

sky   sky

110

Words About Nature

Directions: Write the missing letter or letters for each word. The first one is done for you.

 tree   tree

 grass   grass

 flower   flower

pond   pond

sand   sand

sky   sky

111

Words About Nature

Directions: The letters in each word are mixed up. Unscramble the letters and write each word correctly.

 etre   tree

srags   grass

loefwr   flower

 dnop   pond

 dnsa   sand

 yks   sky

112

Shape Words

A **square** is a figure with four corners and four sides of the same length. This is a square: ☐

Directions: Circle the squares. Then, trace and write the word. Color the picture.

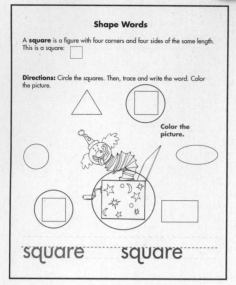

Color the picture.

square   square

113

Words That Are Prepositions

A **preposition** is a word that shows a connection between a noun or pronoun and another word. **Up** and **down** are prepositions.

Directions: Trace and write the preposition words. Then, circle the word that completes each sentence. Write it on the line.

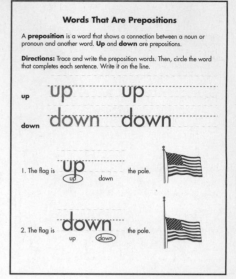

up   up   up

down   DOWN   down

1. The flag is _up_ the pole.
   up   down

2. The flag is _down_ the pole.
   up   down

114

Words That Are Prepositions

Directions: Look at each picture. Circle the correct preposition for each sentence. Write it on the line. Then, color the pictures.

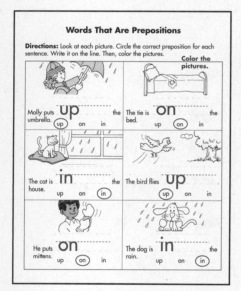

Color the pictures.

Molly puts _up_ the umbrella.
up   on   in

The tie is _on_ the bed.
up   on   in

The cat is _in_ the house.
up   on   in

The bird flies _up_
up   on   in

He puts _on_ mittens.
up   on   in

The dog is _in_ the rain.
up   on   in

115

Words That Are Prepositions

Directions: Read each sentence. Draw the sheep where it belongs. Then, color the pictures.

The sheep is on the table.

Color the pictures.

The sheep is under the loom.

The sheep is in the berry bush.

The sheep is beside the cloth.

The sheep is on Charlie's hat.

The sheep is between the pieces of Charlie's cloak.

116

Words About Historical Figures

Abraham Lincoln was born in a log cabin. He became the 16th president of the United States of America. He is known for his top hat and his beard.

Directions: Use the words in the Word Bank to fill in the lines next to each picture. Then, color the pictures.

Color the pictures.

Word Bank		
log cabin	top hat	ax
White House	book	beard

log cabin
ax
book

Abraham Lincoln as a boy

top hat
White House
beard

Abraham Lincoln as president

117

Words About Plants

Directions: Use the words in the Word Bank to label each plant part. Read about the job of each plant part. Then, follow the directions to color the plant.

Word Bank	
roots	stem
flower	leaf

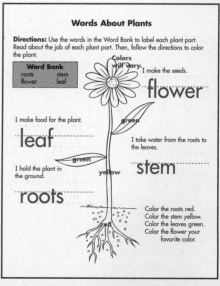

Colors will vary.

I make the seeds.

flower

I make food for the plant.

leaf

I take water from the roots to the leaves.

stem

I hold the plant in the ground.

roots

Color the roots red.
Color the stem yellow.
Color the leaves green.
Color the flower your favorite color.

118

Words About Flowers

Directions: Read about flowers. Then, write the answers.

Some flowers grow in pots. Many flowers grow in flower beds. Others grow beside the road. Flowers begin as seeds. They grow into small buds. Then, they open wide and bloom. Flowers are pretty!

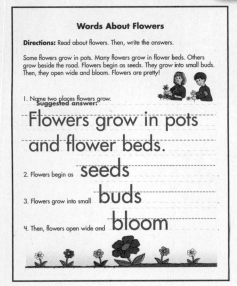

1. Name two places flowers grow.
   Suggested answer:
   Flowers grow in pots and flower beds.

2. Flowers begin as **seeds**

3. Flowers grow into small **buds**

4. Then, flowers open wide and **bloom**

119

Words About Flowers

Directions: Use the words in the Word Bank to complete the puzzle about flowers.

Across
2. Flowers do this when they open wide.
3. Flowers grow from these.

Down
1. A flower can grow in a flower bed or a ___.
2. Before they bloom, flowers grow___.

Word Bank
seeds   pot
bloom   buds

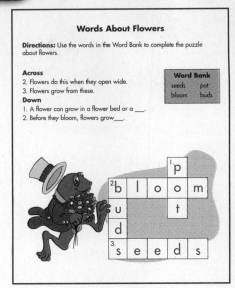

Crossword:
- ¹p
- ²b l o o m
- u / t
- d
- ³s e e d s

120

Shape Words

A **circle** is a figure that is round. This is a circle: ○

Directions: Draw squares around the circles. Then, trace and write the word. Color the picture.

Color the picture.

circle   circle

121

Words for Similarities and Differences

Reading to find out how things are **alike** or **different** can help you picture and remember what you read. Things that are alike are called **similarities**. Things that are not alike are called **differences**.

Similarity: Beth and Michelle are both girls.
Difference: Beth has short hair, but Michelle has long hair.

Directions: Read the story. Then, color the dresses to show how they are alike and different.

Michelle and Beth are wearing new dresses. Both dresses are striped and have four buttons. Each dress has a belt and a pocket. Beth's dress is blue and white, while Michelle's is yellow and white. The stripes on Beth's dress go up and down. Stripes on Michelle's dress go from side to side. Beth's pocket is bigger with room for a kitten.

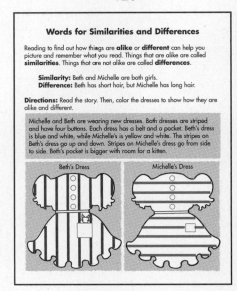

Beth's Dress   Michelle's Dress

122

Words About Historical Figures

Sally Ride was the first American woman in space.

Directions: Trace and write the words. Then, color the picture.

Sally Ride   Sally Ride
woman   woman
space   space

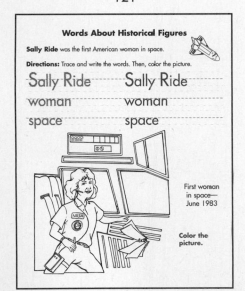

First woman in space—June 1983

Color the picture.

125

Words About Plants

Directions: Use the words in the Word Bank to write the correct plant word under each picture.

Word Bank
pumpkin   seed   sprout   flower   plant

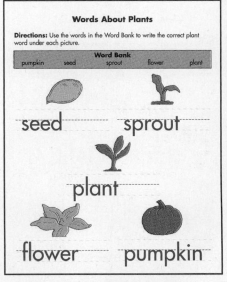

seed   sprout

plant

flower   pumpkin

126

Words About Seeds

Seeds travel from one place to another. Sometimes people move the seeds. Sometimes they are moved in other ways.

Word Bank
people
animals
animals
wind
water

Directions: Use the words in the word bank to finish the sentences to tell how seeds travel.

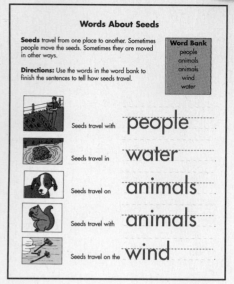

Seeds travel with **people**

Seeds travel in **water**

Seeds travel on **animals**

Seeds travel with **animals**

Seeds travel on the **wind**

127

Words About Seeds

Plants have seeds. Some plants have one seed. Other plants have many seeds. When the seeds are planted, they grow into new plants.

Word Bank
pine
corn
peach
bean

Directions: Use the words in the Word Bank to write the correct plant name under each picture. Count the seeds. Write the number of seeds beside the box. Then, draw a line from each seed to the correct plant.

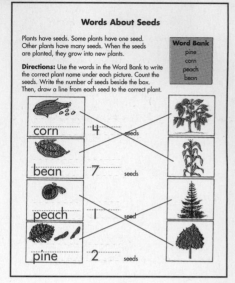

corn — 4 seeds
bean — 7 seeds
peach — 1 seed
pine — 2 seeds

128

Unit 5 Review

Directions: Circle the preposition word in each row.

1. tree (above) beard
2. leaf space (inside)
3. (under) grass wind
4. different seeds (down)
5. square (on) sky
6. (in) roots people

Directions: Write a sentence to tell how Abraham Lincoln and Martin Luther King, Jr. are similar. Then, write a sentence to tell how they are different.

Sentences will vary.

129

Words That Are Opposites

Opposites are things that are different in every way.

Directions: Draw a line from each word to its opposite.

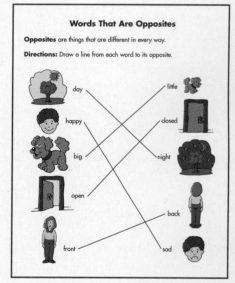

day — little
happy — closed
big — night
open — back
front — sad

131

Words That Are Opposites

Directions: Read each sentence and look at the first picture in each row. Then, look at the next picture. Use a word in the Word Bank to write a sentence that tells about it. The first one is done for you.

Word Bank
found   new   big   last

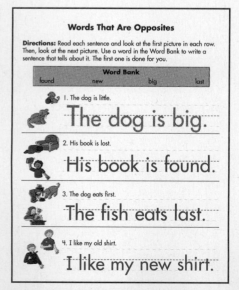

1. The dog is little.
The dog is big.

2. His book is lost.
His book is found.

3. The dog eats first.
The fish eats last.

4. I like my old shirt.
I like my new shirt.

132

Words That Are Opposites

Directions: Find the object in the picture that shows the opposite of each word. Write the object on the line.

Answers may vary.

1. low **bird**   4. short **tree**

2. cold **sun**   5. noisy **dog**

3. dry **pool**   6. hard **grass**

133

Words About Historical Figures

George Washington was the first president of the United States of America. He appears on the dollar bill.

Directions: Connect the dots, beginning with number 1.
Color the dollar bill.

Color the picture. Then write: George Washington was our first president.

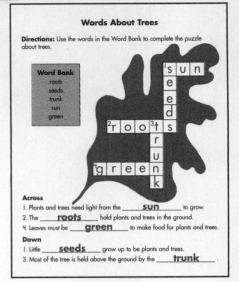

George Washington
was our first president.

134

Words About Trees

Directions: Use the words in the Word Bank to complete the puzzle about trees.

Word Bank
roots
seeds
trunk
sun
green

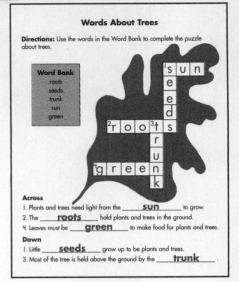

Across
1. Plants and trees need light from the **sun** to grow.
2. The **roots** hold plants and trees in the ground.
4. Leaves must be **green** to make food for plants and trees.

Down
1. Little **seeds** grow up to be plants and trees.
3. Most of the tree is held above the ground by the **trunk**.

135

Words About Leaves

Leaves make food for trees. Leaves use sunlight to make food. In the fall, they drop to the ground. You can find many shapes and colors of leaves.

Directions: Go outside. Compare the leaves you find with the leaves below. Circle the leaves that look like those you find. Color the leaves on this page.

Answers will vary.

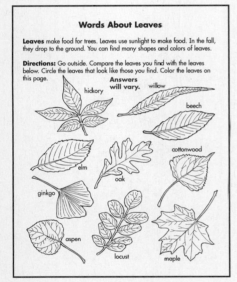

hickory
willow
beech
cottonwood
elm
oak
ginkgo
aspen
locust
maple

136

Words About Leaves

Leaves are like little factories. They make food for the tree. Leaves need sunshine, air, and water to make food.

Leaves change in the fall. They lose their green color. Then, they cannot make food for the tree.

Directions: On the left side of the box, draw a leaf that can make food. Color it green.
On the right side of the box, draw a leaf that cannot make food. Color it red.
Circle the correct word for each sentence. Write it on the line.

green leaf	red leaf

1. Food is made by **green** (green) yellow leaves.

2. Leaves need **sunshine** shade (sunshine) to make food.

3. Leaves **cannot** can (cannot) make food in the fall.

137

Shape Words

A **rectangle** is a figure with four corners and four sides. The sides opposite each other are the same length.
This is a rectangle:

Directions: Circle each rectangle. Then, trace and write the word.

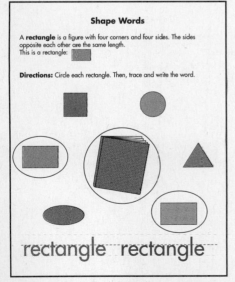

rectangle rectangle

138

Words That Are Opposites

Directions: Color the spaces yellow if they have word pairs with opposite meanings.
Color the spaces blue if they have word pairs with similar meanings.

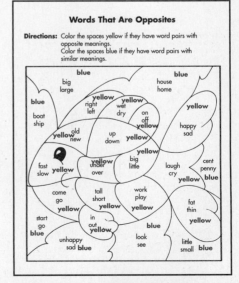

blue — big large
blue — house home
blue — boat ship
yellow — right left
yellow — wet dry
yellow — on off
yellow
blue
yellow — old new
yellow — up down
yellow
happy sad
yellow
fast slow
yellow
yellow — under over
yellow — big little
laugh cry
cent penny
yellow
blue
come go
tall short
work play
fat thin
yellow
yellow
yellow
start go
blue
in out
yellow
blue
yellow
unhappy sad
blue
look see
little small
blue

139

Words That Are Opposites

Directions: Use the words in the Word Bank to complete the puzzle about opposites.

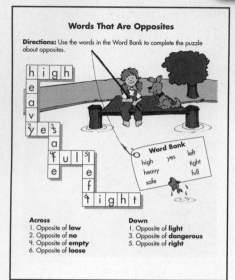

Word Bank

high   yes   left
heavy   tight
safe   full

Across
1. Opposite of **low**
2. Opposite of **no**
4. Opposite of **empty**
6. Opposite of **loose**

Down
1. Opposite of **light**
3. Opposite of **dangerous**
5. Opposite of **right**

140

Words That Are Opposites

Some words are opposites. **Opposites** are things that are different in every way. **Dark** and **light** are opposites.

Directions: Trace and write the words. The first one is done for you.

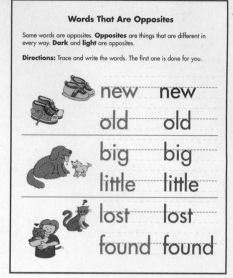

new   new
old   old
big   big
little little
lost   lost
found found

141

Words About Historical Figures

The first thirteen states to make up the United States began as **colonies**. **Colonists** were the people who lived in or were members of the colonies. They had many different jobs.

Directions: Draw shoes in the window for the shoemaker.
Draw dough for the baker to make bread.
Draw a hammer in the blacksmith's hand.
Draw a dress on the hanger for the dressmaker.
Draw a saddle for the saddlemaker.
Draw sacks of flour and sugar for the storekeeper.

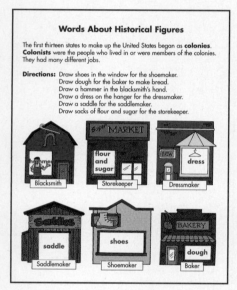

142

Words About Trees

Trees have three main parts: the trunk, the roots, and the leaves. Each part has a special job.

Directions: Cut out the name of each tree part. Cut out the job of each part. Glue them onto the picture in their correct places.

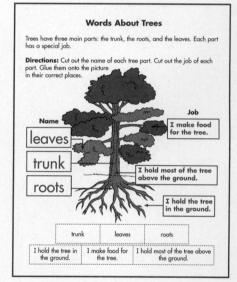

Name
leaves
trunk
roots

Job
I make food for the tree.
I hold most of the tree above the ground.
I hold the tree in the ground.

trunk	leaves	roots
I hold the tree in the ground.	I make food for the tree.	I hold most of the tree above the ground.

143

Words About Trees

Some trees drop their seeds in the spring. Other trees drop their seeds in the fall. The seeds grow up. Do you know what they grow up to be?

Directions: Write **first**, **second**, or **third** under each picture to show how the acorn grows into a mighty oak tree. Color the pictures. Then, complete the sentence below.

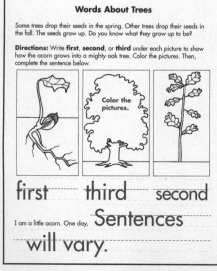

Color the pictures.

first   third   second

I am a little acorn. One day, Sentences
will vary.

145

Shape Words

A **triangle** is a figure with three corners and three sides. This is a triangle:

Directions: Circle each triangle. Then, trace and write the word.

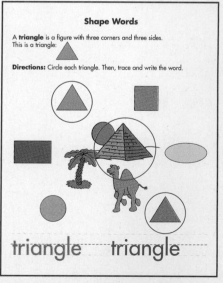

triangle   triangle

146

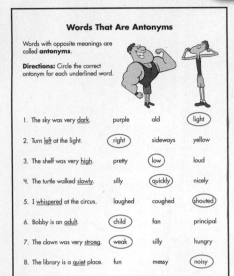

Words That Are Antonyms

Words with opposite meanings are called **antonyms**.

Directions: Circle the correct antonym for each underlined word.

1. The sky was very dark.   purple   old   (light)
2. Turn left at the light.   (right)   sideways   yellow
3. The shelf was very high.   pretty   (low)   loud
4. The turtle walked slowly.   silly   (quickly)   nicely
5. I whispered at the circus.   laughed   coughed   (shouted)
6. Bobby is an adult.   (child)   fan   principal
7. The clown was very strong.   (weak)   silly   hungry
8. The library is a quiet place.   fun   messy   (noisy)

147

Words That Are Antonyms

Antonyms are words that have opposite meanings. **Old** and **new** are antonyms. **Laugh** and **cry** are antonyms, too.

Directions: Use the words in the Word Bank to write the correct antonym under each picture.

Word Bank
down
go
left
sad
dry

stop — **go**
happy — **sad**
right — **left**
up — **down**
wet — **dry**

148

Words That Are Antonyms

Directions: Look at each picture. Then, write the answer to the question.

Example: Is the cookie big?

No, the cookie is little.

1. Has the boy found his boat?

No, the boy has lost his boat.

2. Will he go first?

No, he will go last.

3. Is the sky dark?

No, the sky is light.

149

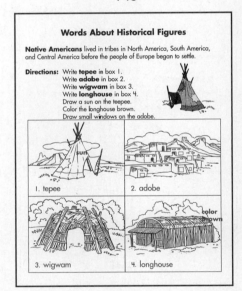

Words About Historical Figures

Native Americans lived in tribes in North America, South America, and Central America before the people of Europe began to settle.

Directions: Write **tepee** in box 1.
Write **adobe** in box 2.
Write **wigwam** in box 3.
Write **longhouse** in box 4.
Draw a sun on the teepee.
Color the longhouse brown.
Draw small windows on the adobe.

1. tepee   2. adobe
3. wigwam   4. longhouse

150

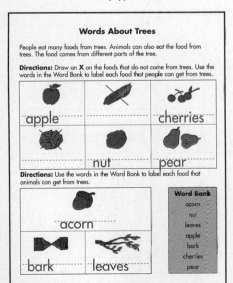

Words About Trees

People eat many foods from trees. Animals can also eat the food from trees. The food comes from different parts of the tree.

Directions: Draw an **X** on the foods that do not come from trees. Use the words in the Word Bank to label each food that people can get from trees.

apple   cherries
nut   pear

Directions: Use the words in the Word Bank to label each food that animals can get from trees.

acorn
bark   leaves

Word Bank
acorn
nut
leaves
apple
bark
cherries
pear

151

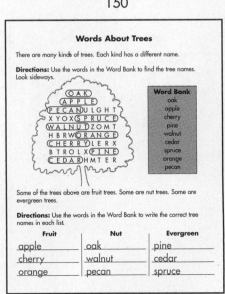

Words About Trees

There are many kinds of trees. Each kind has a different name.

Directions: Use the words in the Word Bank to find the tree names. Look sideways.

Word Bank
oak
apple
cherry
pine
walnut
cedar
spruce
orange
pecan

Some of the trees above are fruit trees. Some are nut trees. Some are evergreen trees.

Directions: Use the words in the Word Bank to write the correct tree names in each list.

Fruit	Nut	Evergreen
apple	oak	pine
cherry	walnut	cedar
orange	pecan	spruce

152

Words About Plants

We eat many plant parts. Sometimes, we eat just the fruit. Sometimes, we eat just the leaves. We also might eat the stem, the root, or the seeds.

Directions: Draw a line from each plant part to its name. Then, color the plant parts. The first one is done for you.

— stem

— leaf

— root

— seed

— fruit

153

Unit 6 Review

Directions: Read each sentence. The underlined word makes the sentence wrong. Write the opposite of the word to correct each sentence.

1. I was happy when I lost my dog.   sad
2. It is hot in the winter.   cold
3. You must be noisy in the library.   quiet
4. George Washington was our last president.   first
5. Leaves need moonlight to make food.   sunshine
6. His glass was empty after he poured milk in it.   full
7. It is dangerous to wear a helmet when you ride a bike.   safe
8. Seeds grow down to become big trees.   up
9. A turtle walks quickly.   slowly
10. Leaves can make food for the tree when they lose their green color.   cannot

154

Words That Are Synonyms

Synonyms are words that have almost the same meaning. **Tired** and **sleepy** are synonyms. **Talk** and **speak** are synonyms.

Directions: Read each word. Use the words on the anthill to write the correct synonym on each line.

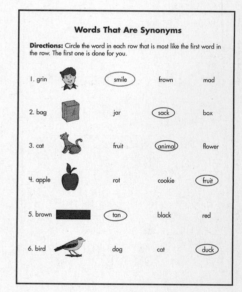

1. glad   happy
2. little   small
3. begin   start
4. above   over
5. damp   wet
6. large   big

156

Words That Are Synonyms

Directions: Circle the word in each row that is most like the first word in the row. The first one is done for you.

1. grin   (smile)   frown   mad
2. bag   jar   (sack)   box
3. cat   fruit   (animal) flower
4. apple   rot   cookie   (fruit)
5. brown   (tan)   black   red
6. bird   dog   cat   (duck)

157

Words That Are Synonyms

Directions: Read the story. Use the words in the Word Bank to write the correct synonym on each line.

Word Bank
market
ran   fruit
coins fast

Dan went to the   market
                    store

He wanted to buy   fruit
                    food

He walked very   fast
                    quickly

The store had what he wanted.

He bought it using   coins
                     dimes

Instead of walking, Dan   ran
                           jogged

158

Holiday Words

The pilgrims celebrated their first harvest with the Native Americans who had helped them. This celebration became known as **Thanksgiving**.

Directions: Use the words in the Word Bank to find the hidden foods. Then, color the picture.

Color the picture.

| corn | pumpkin | squash | turkey |
| onion | beans | berries | fish |

159

Food Words

Directions: Trace and write the food words. Then, color the pictures. The first one is done for you.

Color the pictures.

bread   bread
cookie   cookie
apple   apple
cake   cake
milk   milk
egg   egg

160

Food Words

Directions: Complete each sentence with the correct food word. Use the pictures to help you.

Kim got up in the morning.

"Do you want an egg ?" her mother asked.

"Yes, please," Kim said.

"May I have some milk , too?"

"Okay," her mother said.

"How about some ice cream ?" Kim asked.

Her mother laughed. "Not now," she said.

She put an apple in Kim's lunch.

"Do you want a cookie or some cake today?"

"Both!" Kim said.

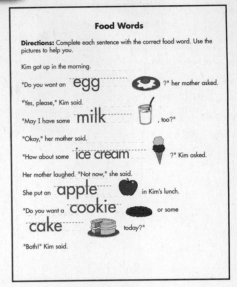

161

Food Words

Directions: Use the words in the Word Bank to complete the puzzle about food.

Across
3. It comes from cows.
5. It can go in a pie.
7. It is good with jelly.

Down
1. It is brown and sweet.
2. Rabbits like them.
4. It is made from milk.
6. It can be red, yellow, or green.
8. It is yellow and grows in a bunch.

Word Bank
apple   peanut butter   cheese   carrots
cherry   raisin   milk   banana

162

Shape Words

An **oval** is an egg-shaped figure. This is an oval:

A **diamond** is a figure with four sides of the same length. Its corners form points at the top, sides, and bottom. This is a diamond:

Directions: Color the ovals red. Color the diamonds blue. Then, trace and write the words.

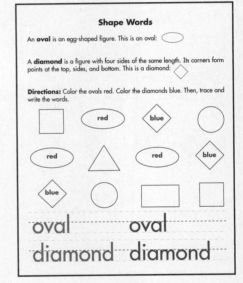

oval   oval
diamond   diamond

163

Words That Are Synonyms

Synonyms are words that mean almost the same thing. **Start** and **begin** are synonyms.

Directions: Look at each picture. Use the words in the Word Bank to write the correct synonyms in each box.

small   funny   large   sad   silly   little   big   unhappy

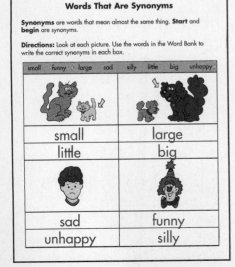

small   large
little   big
sad   funny
unhappy   silly

164

Words That Are Synonyms

Directions: Look at each picture. Use the words in the Word Bank to write the correct synonyms in each box.

Word Bank
rocks   start   road   begin   street   stones   sad   unhappy

sad   rocks
unhappy   stones
road   start
street   begin

165

Words That Are Synonyms

Directions: Circle the synonym in each square that has the same meaning or close to the same meaning as the word in bold print. The first one is done for you.

end **start**	⟨scream⟩ **shout**	cat **sick**
⟨begin⟩	brother	bath
stop	talk	⟨ill⟩

Directions: Think of a synonym for each of the three words listed. Then, write a sentence using both words.

1. smart/ Words will vary.
   Sentences will vary.

2. bad/

3. little/

166

Holiday Words

Holidays begin with capital letters.

Directions: Use the words in the Word Bank to write the correct holiday name under each picture.

Word Bank

Fourth of July	Valentine's Day
Presidents' Day	Thanksgiving

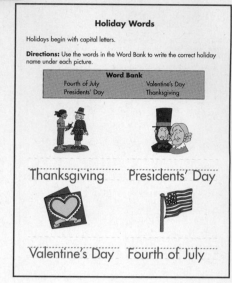

Thanksgiving   Presidents' Day

Valentine's Day   Fourth of July

167

Food Words

Fruit comes from plants. It is sweet.

Directions: Look at each picture and food word. Then, write the names of the fruits on the lines.

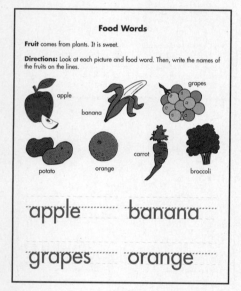

apple   banana

grapes   orange

168

Food Words

Vegetables grow in gardens. Vegetables help to keep people healthy.

Directions: Look at each picture and food word. Then, write the names of the vegetables on the lines. Think of one more vegetable to add on the last line.

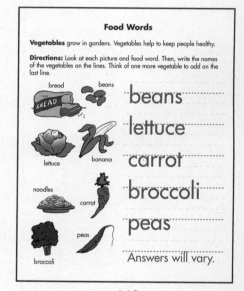

beans
lettuce
carrot
broccoli
peas
Answers will vary.

169

Drink Words

Directions: Circle the pictures of things you can drink. Then, write the names of those things on the lines.

milk

juice   soda

170

Shape Words

Directions: Use the words in the Word Bank to find the shape words. Look up, down, and sideways. Then, color the shapes.

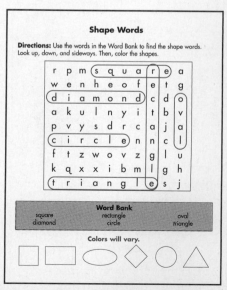

Word Bank

square	rectangle	oval
diamond	circle	triangle

Colors will vary.

171

Words That Are Synonyms

Directions: Read each sentence. Use the words in the Word Bank to write the correct synonym for each underlined word. The first one is done for you.

Word Bank

pick   tired
porch   pull

1. I was so <u>sleepy</u> I couldn't wait to go to bed! **tired**

2. Please <u>choose</u> a present you would like to open. **pick**

3. Are you strong enough to <u>drag</u> this heavy crate? **pull**

4. We sipped lemonade on the <u>deck</u>. **porch**

172

Words That Are Synonyms

Directions: Read each sentence. Circle the correct synonym for each underlined word. Then, write the new words on the lines.

1. The boy was <u>mad</u>.   happy   (angry)   pup
2. The <u>dog</u> is brown.   (pup)   cat   rat
3. I like to <u>scream</u>.   soar   mad   (shout)
4. The bird can <u>fly</u>.   (soar)   jog   warm
5. The girl can <u>run</u>.   sleep   (jog)   shout
6. I am <u>hot</u>.   (warm)   cold   soar

angry   pup   shout

soar   jog   warm

173

Words That Are Synonyms

Directions: Use the words in the Word Bank to write the correct synonym on each line.

Word Bank

bright   hop   dad   fast
pretty   plate   silly   center

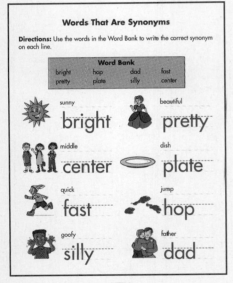

sunny **bright**

beautiful **pretty**

middle **center**

dish **plate**

quick **fast**

jump **hop**

goofy **silly**

father **dad**

174

Words About Voting

To **vote** is to express a choice in a decision. In the United States of America, people vote on many different things. People decide on the president by voting.

Directions: Senators represent people from different areas of the country. They vote on many issues. Write a letter to your state senator about a problem you would like him or her to solve.

(date)

(address)

Dear Senator _____,

Letters will vary.

Sincerely,

175

Food Words

Directions: Draw a meal you like to eat. Draw one meat, one fruit or vegetable, one bread, and one dairy food. Then, answer the questions.

Pictures will vary.

1. What is your meat? **Answers will vary.**

2. What is your fruit or vegetable?

3. What is your bread?

4. What is your dairy food?

176

Food Words

Directions: Use the words in the Word Bank to write the correct food in each food group.

Word Bank

ham   bagel   pear
bean   pie   yogurt

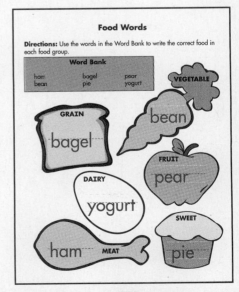

VEGETABLE **bean**

GRAIN **bagel**

FRUIT **pear**

DAIRY **yogurt**

MEAT **ham**

SWEET **pie**

177

Food Words

Directions: Use the words in the Word Bank to write the correct food names in each food group.

Word Bank

carrots	cherries	chicken	cheese	fish	ham
cake	lettuce	bagel	oranges	pears	rolls
	beans	toast	pie	yogurt	
	cottage cheese		candy bar		

Dairy
cheese
yogurt
cottage cheese

Meats
ham
fish
chicken

Fruits
pears
cherries
oranges

Sweets
pie
cake
candy bar

Vegetables
beans
carrots
lettuce

Grains
toast
bagel
rolls

178

Unit 7 Review

Directions: Draw a line from each word to its synonym.

start — jog
dish — little
small — begin
run — tired
sleepy — plate

Directions: The letters in each word are mixed up. Unscramble the letters and write each word correctly.

1. catorr   carrot
2. daber   bread
3. epalp   apple
4. ipe   pie
5. heseec   cheese

Directions: Write the holiday word correctly.

thanksgiving   Thanksgiving

179

Compound Words

Some short words can be put together to make one new word. The new word is called a **compound word**.

Example: cow + boy = cowboy

Directions: Look at each pair of pictures and words. Join together the two words to make a compound word. Write it on the line.

rain + coat =   raincoat
door + bell =   doorbell
dog + house =   doghouse
pan + cake =   pancake
horse + shoe =   horseshoe

181

Compound Words

Directions: Write the two words that make up each compound word.

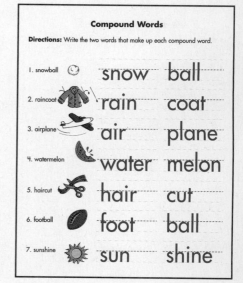

1. snowball   snow ball
2. raincoat   rain coat
3. airplane   air plane
4. watermelon   water melon
5. haircut   hair cut
6. football   foot ball
7. sunshine   sun shine

182

Compound Words

Directions: Underline the two words in each sentence that can make a compound word. Write the compound word on the line to complete the sentence.

A kind of bird that is black is a
blackbird

A horse that can race is a
racehorse

A cloth that covers a table is a
tablecloth

A room with a bed is a
bedroom

A book with a story is a
storybook

A bowl that holds a fish is a
fishbowl

183

People Words

Directions: Trace and write the people words.

girl   girl
boy   boy
man   man
woman   woman
people   people
children   children

184

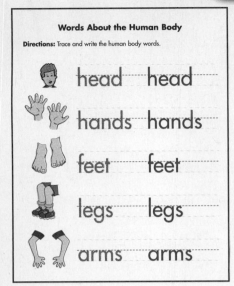

Words About the Human Body

Directions: Trace and write the human body words.

head   head

hands   hands

feet   feet

legs   legs

arms   arms

185

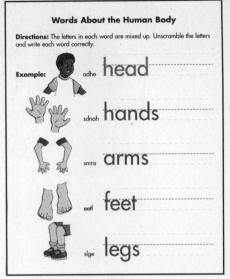

Words About the Human Body

Directions: The letters in each word are mixed up. Unscramble the letters and write each word correctly.

Example: adhe   head

sdnah   hands

smra   arms

eetf   feet

slge   legs

186

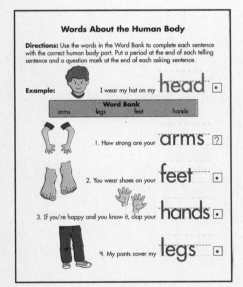

Words About the Human Body

Directions: Use the words in the Word Bank to complete each sentence with the correct human body part. Put a period at the end of each telling sentence and a question mark at the end of each asking sentence.

Example: I wear my hat on my   head   .

Word Bank
arms   legs   feet   hands

1. How strong are your   arms   ?

2. You wear shoes on your   feet   .

3. If you're happy and you know it, clap your   hands   .

4. My pants cover my   legs   .

187

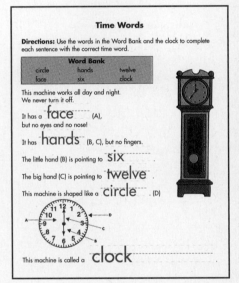

Time Words

Directions: Use the words in the Word Bank and the clock to complete each sentence with the correct time word.

Word Bank
| circle | hands | twelve |
| face | six | clock |

This machine works all day and night. We never turn it off.

It has a   face   (A), but no eyes and no nose!

It has   hands   (B, C), but no fingers.

The little hand (B) is pointing to   six

The big hand (C) is pointing to   twelve

This machine is shaped like a   circle   . (D)

This machine is called a   clock

188

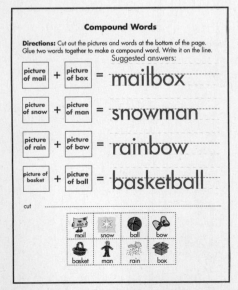

Compound Words

Directions: Cut out the pictures and words at the bottom of the page. Glue two words together to make a compound word. Write it on the line.
Suggested answers:

picture of mail	+	picture of box	=	mailbox
picture of snow	+	picture of man	=	snowman
picture of rain	+	picture of bow	=	rainbow
picture of basket	+	picture of ball	=	basketball

cut

mail   snow   ball   bow

basket   man   rain   box

189

333

Compound Words

Directions: Draw lines to make compound words. Write the new words on the lines.

Example: song + bird = songbird

dog   room
foot   box
bed   house
mail   light
some   ball
moon   thing

doghouse   mailbox
football   something
bedroom   moonlight

191

People Words

Directions: Complete each sentence with the correct people word. Use the pictures to help you.

1. The **boy** was last in line at the toy store.

2. The **children** took a walk in the woods.

3. The **girl** had to help her father.

4. The **woman** had a surprise for the children.

5. Some **people** like to eat outside.

6. Something came out of the box when the **man** opened it.

192

Words About the Human Body

Directions: Read the two sentences on each line. Draw a line between them. Then, write each sentence again. Begin each sentence with a capital letter. Put a period at the end of each telling sentence and a question mark at the end of each asking sentence.

Example: wash your hands I they are dirty

Wash your hands.
They are dirty.

1. you have big arms|are you very strong

You have big arms.
Are you very strong?

2. I have two feet|I can run fast

I have two feet.
I can run fast.

193

Words About the Human Body

Directions: Use the words in the Word Bank to answer each riddle.

Word Bank				
eyes	hair	mouth	nose	skin

1. There are two of me. We can blink. We can see. We can wink. We can weep.

   What are we? **eyes**

2. There is one of me. I can sing. I can speak. I can eat. I can even blow a big bubble. I can eat ice cream, too.

   What am I? **mouth**

3. There is one of me. If something tickles me, I will sneeze. I like to sniff flowers. I like the smell of hot dogs, also.

   What am I? **nose**

4. I can be almost any color. I can be long or short. I can be curled and I can be straight.

   What am I? **hair**

5. I cover a lot. I keep muscles, bones, and blood inside your body. I let you know if it is hot or cold outside. I tell you if something is wet or dry.

   What am I? **skin**

194

Words About the Human Body

Directions: Use the words in the Word Bank to find the human body words. Look up, down, and sideways.

Word Bank				
head	arm	foot	brain	skeleton
bone	skin	blood	heart	windpipe
lungs	eye	muscle	teeth	stomach

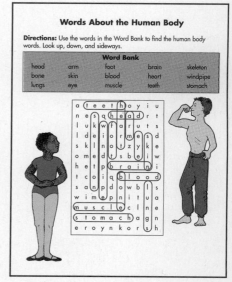

195

Time Words

There are many ways to measure time. A **year** has 365 days in it. A **week** has 7 days in it. A **day** has 24 hours in it. An **hour** has 60 minutes in it. A **minute** has 60 seconds in it. A **second** goes very quickly.

Directions: Use the words in the Word Bank to complete the puzzle about time.

Word Bank				
day	year	minute	week	hour

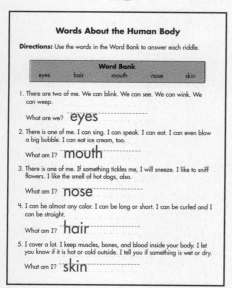

1. ↓ 365 days make a y **ear**
2. → 7 days make a w **eek**
3. → 24 hours make a d **ay**
4. → 60 minutes make an h **our**
5. ↓ 60 seconds make a m **inute**

196

Compound Words

Directions: Use the words in the Word Bank to complete each sentence with the correct compound word.

Word Bank				
raincoat	bedroom	lunchbox	hallway	sandbox

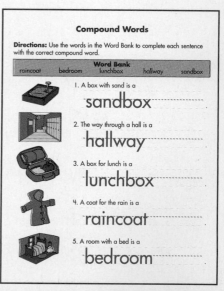

1. A box with sand is a **sandbox**

2. The way through a hall is a **hallway**

3. A box for lunch is a **lunchbox**

4. A coat for the rain is a **raincoat**

5. A room with a bed is a **bedroom**

199

People Words

Directions: Use the words in the Word Bank to find the people words. Look up, down, and sideways. One is done for you.

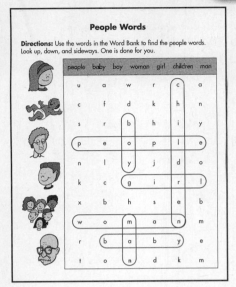

| people | baby | boy | woman | girl | children | man |

u	a	w	r	c	a
c	f	d	k	h	n
s	r	b	h	i	y
p	e	o	p	l	e
n	l	y	j	d	o
k	c	g	i	r	l
x	b	h	s	e	b
w	o	m	a	n	m
r	b	a	b	y	e
t	o	n	d	k	m

200

Words About the Human Body

Bones give your body shape. They help you stand up tall. You cannot see your bones. But you can feel many of your bones under your skin.

Directions: Draw a line from each bone to the part of the body where it is found. Use the words in the Word Bank to label each bone.

Word Bank
| skull | ribs | foot |
| hand | knee | hips |

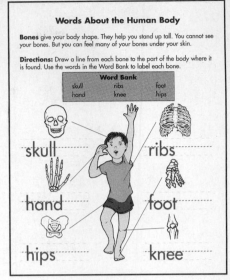

skull   ribs

hand   foot

hips   knee

201

Words About the Human Body

Directions: Use the words in the Word Bank to complete the puzzle about the human body.

Across
3. They protect your heart and lungs.
6. All of your bones.
7. It connects your leg and foot.

Down
1. Found on the end of your hands.
2. Found on the end of your feet.
4. Your spine.
5. It makes your leg bend.
6. This protects your brain.

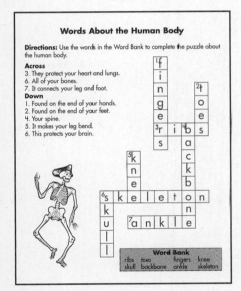

Crossword answers:
1. fingers (down)
2. toes (down)
3. ribs (across)
4. backbone (down)
5. knee (down)
6. skeleton (across) / skull (down)
7. ankle (across)

Word Bank
| ribs | toes | | fingers | knee |
| skull | backbone | ankle | | skeleton |

202

Words About the Human Body

Directions: Use the words at the bottom of the page to complete the puzzle about the human body.

Across
2. You use these to breathe.
4. You need to do this when you're tired.
5. This breaks down food.
7. This tells your body what to do.
9. This is a gas you breathe.
10. It pumps blood.

Down
1. It carries oxygen to your body.
3. Tiny living things that can make you sick.
6. This helps you when you are sick.
8. These support and shape your body.

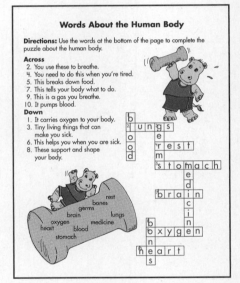

Crossword answers:
1. blood (down)
2. lungs (across)
3. germs (down)
4. rest (across)
5. stomach (across)
6. medicine (down)
7. brain (across)
8. bones (down)
9. oxygen (across)
10. heart (across)

rest
bones
germs
brain   lungs
oxygen   medicine
heart   blood
stomach

203

Unit 8 Review

Directions: Use a word in the Word Bank to write a complete sentence about your body.

Word Bank
| rib | arm | bone | muscle | knee | nose |

Sentences will vary.

Directions: Use the words in the Word Bank to write six compound words.

Word Bank
| pan | rain | ball | bed | coat | sun |
| cake | mail | foot | room | shine | box |

Suggested answers:
1. pancake
2. raincoat
3. football
4. sunshine
5. bedroom
6. mailbox

Directions: Use the words in the Word Bank to write the time words in order from the least amount of time to the most.

Word Bank
| day | year | minute | week | hour |

1. minute
2. hour
3. day
4. week
5. year

204

Words That Are Homophones

Homophones are words that sound the same but have different spellings and meanings. **Too** and **two** are homophones. So are **road** and **rode**.

Directions: Color the balloons yellow that have homophones.

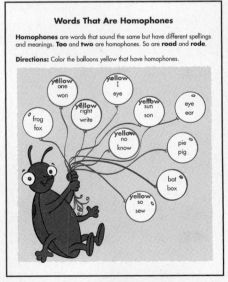

yellow one won
yellow I
yellow right write
yellow sun son
yellow eye
frog fox
yellow no know
eye ear
pie pig
bat box
yellow so sew

206

335

Words That Are Homophones

Directions: Read each sentence. Underline the two words that sound the same but are spelled differently and mean something different.

1. Tom <u>ate</u> <u>eight</u> grapes.

2. Becky <u>read</u> Little <u>Red</u> Riding Hood.

3. I went <u>to</u> buy <u>two</u> dolls.

4. Five <u>blue</u> feathers <u>blew</u> in the wind.

5. <u>Would</u> you get <u>wood</u> for the fire?

207

Words That Are Homophones

Directions: Complete each sentence with the correct homophone.

to · two

1. Jim	**ate**	the cookies.	ate / eight
2. Sally has	**two**	pencils.	to / two
3. The	**road**	is bumpy.	rode / road
4.	**I**	can ride a bike.	Eye / I
5. Can you	**see**	the picture?	see / sea
6. Tom	**blew**	up the balloon.	blew / blue

208

People Words

Directions: Trace and write the people words. Then, circle the correct people word for each sentence. Write it on the line.

you and me you and me

you and me

1. I will play with **you** — (you) me

2. You can go with **me** — you (me)

3. Can you run with **me** ? — you (me)

209

Sense Words

Directions: Trace and write the sense words.

Example:

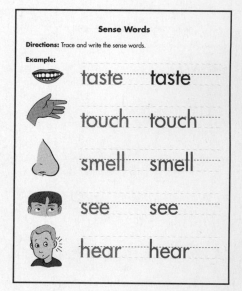

taste taste

touch touch

smell smell

see see

hear hear

210

Sense Words

Directions: Circle the word in each row that is spelled correctly. Write it on the line.

Example:

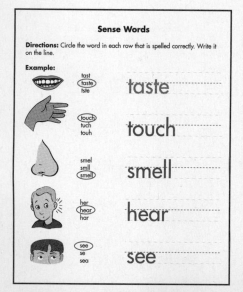

tast / (taste) / tste — taste

(touch) / tuch / touh — touch

smel / smll / (smell) — smell

her / (hear) / har — hear

(see) / se / sea — see

211

Sense Words

Directions: Complete each sentence with the correct sense word. The first one is done for you.

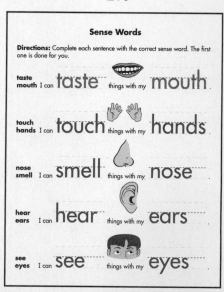

taste / mouth — I can **taste** things with my **mouth**

touch / hands — I can **touch** things with my **hands**

nose / smell — I can **smell** things with my **nose**

hear / ears — I can **hear** things with my **ears**

see / eyes — I can **see** things with my **eyes**

212

Time Words

The days of the week begin with capital letters.

Directions: Use the words in the Word Bank to write the days of the week in the correct order on the lines.

Word Bank	
Tuesday	Sunday
Saturday	Monday
Monday	Tuesday
Friday	Wednesday
Thursday	Thursday
Sunday	Friday
Wednesday	Saturday

213

Words That Are Homonyms

Homonyms are words that have more than one meaning.

Directions: Read each word and its meanings. Then, use the numbers to match each picture with the correct meaning.

cross:
1. to draw a line through
2. angry

fall:
3. the season between summer and winter
4. to trip or stumble

land:
5. to bring to a stop or rest
6. the ground

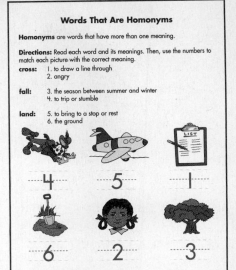

214

Words That Are Homophones

Homophones are words that sound the same but are spelled differently and mean something different. **Blew** and **blue** are homophones.

Directions: Look at the word pairs. Circle the word that describes the picture. Write it on the line.

1. (sew) so   sew
2. pair (pear)   pear
3. (eye) I   eye
4. see (sea)   sea

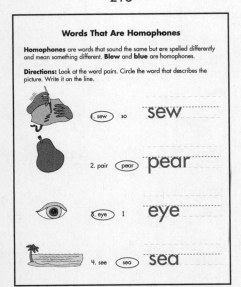

215

Words That Are Homophones

Directions: Circle the word that matches the picture. Then, complete each sentence with the correct word.

1. This is a present **for** your birthday. (four / for)

2. Jane lost a **pair** of new shoes. (pair / pear)

3. The boys will either swim **or** go to the ball game. (oar / or)

4. Let's **meet** at eight o'clock. (meet / meat)

5. Old Mother Hubbard's cupboard was **bare**. (bear / bare)

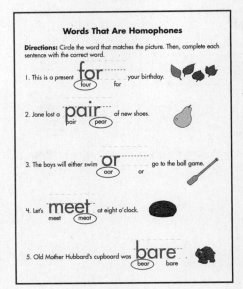

216

People Words

Sometimes we use other words in place of people names. For **boy** or **man**, we can use the word **he**. For **girl** or **woman**, we can use the word **she**. For two or more people, we can use the word **they**.

Directions: Write **he**, **she**, or **they** to complete each sentence.

Example: The boy likes cars. **He** likes cars.

1. The girl is running fast. **She** is running fast.

2. The man looks funny. **He** looks funny.

3. The woman is a teacher. **She** is a teacher.

4. The children like school. **They** like school.

217

Feeling Words

Directions: Use the words in the Word Bank to write the correct feeling words under each picture.

Word Bank		
glad	unhappy	pleased
sorry	sad	happy

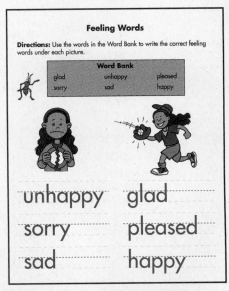

unhappy   glad
sorry   pleased
sad   happy

218

337

Feeling Words

Directions: Read the story. Then, write two different feelings the main character experiences in the story.

> Yesterday, my friend Rex and I visited the museum. We were excited about seeing the new dinosaur display.
> "Wow!" I yelled when I looked up at the tyrannosaurus skeleton.
> "He's my distant cousin," Rex joked. "In fact, I was named after him!"
> "My cousin was really a picky eater," giggled Rex. "He's no skin, just bones!"
> That night, I dreamed of that tyrannosaurus. I imagined him sticking his head into my bedroom window. I was too frightened to scream. When he opened his huge mouth, I froze.
> "Do you know what happened to me because I wouldn't take a bath?" thundered the dinosaur.
> I shook my head.
> "I became x-stinked!" he roared.
> Now, I think that Rex and his dinosaur "cousin" must really be related. They both tell bad jokes!

Words will vary.

219

Feeling Words

Directions: Complete each sentence.

When I feel happy, I

Sentences will vary.

When I feel sad, I

_____

When I feel angry, I

_____

When I feel scared, I

_____

When I feel excited, I

_____

220

Time Words

Directions: Read about the days of the week. Then, answer the questions.

Do you know the names of the seven days of the week? Here they are: Sunday, Monday, Tuesday, Wednesday, Thursday, Friday, and Saturday.

1. What day comes after Thursday?

Friday

2. What day comes before Tuesday?

Monday

3. What day comes after Saturday?

Sunday

4. How many days are in each week?

seven

221

Words That Sound Like Noises

Onomatopoeia is the use of words that sound like the noises they represent. These words can make writing more interesting to read.

Example: The machine **clicked** and **whirred**, but it still did not work. My mother's favorite dish fell to the floor with a **crash**!

Directions: Draw a line from each word to the picture it describes.

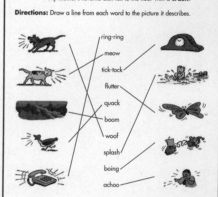

ring-ring
meow
tick-tock
flutter
quack
boom
woof
splash
boing
achoo

222

Figures of Speech

You can make sentences more interesting by using figures of speech. The following are four popular kinds of figures of speech.

Personification—gives human characteristics to things
　Example: The sun touched me with its warm fingers.
Hyperbole—great exaggeration
　Example: She is the happiest person in the universe.
Simile—compares two unlike things using **like** or **as**
　Example: He is as hungry as a horse.
Metaphor—suggests a comparison of two unlike things
　Example: The empty field was a desert.

Directions: Underline the figure of speech in each sentence. Then, write its name on the line.

1. The <u>wind howled</u> as the storm grew closer.

personification

2. The little lady nibbled at her lunch <u>like a bird</u>.

simile

3. Sarah's little sister <u>was a doll</u> in her new clothes.

metaphor

4. The leader said he would <u>never sleep again</u>.

hyperbole

223

Words That Are Palindromes

Directions: Use the words in the Word Bank to write the correct palindrome on each line.

Word Bank				
tot	dad	peep	pup	eye
sees	noon	bib	mom	ewe

1. Sound a chick makes　　**peep**

2. Midday　　**noon**

3. A napkin tied under a baby's chin　　**bib**

4. A little dog　　**pup**

5. Common name for father　　**dad**

6. Watches　　**sees**

7. A female sheep　　**ewe**

8. A seeing organ　　**eye**

9. Short for mother　　**mom**

10. A small child　　**tot**

224

People Words

Word Bank

Dr.	Miss	Mr.	Mrs.

Directions: Use the words in the Word Bank to write a correct title in each address.

1. Dr. or Mr. Tom Brown
   134 Main Street
   New Town, PA

2. Dr., Miss, or Mrs. Mary Wilson
   265 Greenwood Circle
   Dallas, TX

3. Dr. or Mr. Henry Boxer
   1567 West Avenue
   Springdale, VT

4. Dr., Miss, or Mrs. Sally Smith
   901 Club Court
   Brownville, OR

225

Feeling Words

Directions: Check the happy words in the top box. Then, find the checked words hidden in the puzzle. Look up, down, and sideways.

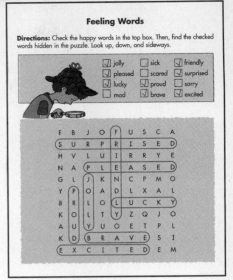

☑ jolly ☐ sick ☑ friendly
☑ pleased ☐ scared ☑ surprised
☑ lucky ☑ proud ☐ sorry
☐ mad ☑ brave ☑ excited

```
F B J O F U S C A
S U R P R I S E D
H V L U I R R Y E
N A P L E A S E D
G L J K N C P M O
Y P O A D L X A L
B R O L O L U C K Y
K O L T Y Z Q J O
A U Y U O E T P L
K D B R A V E S I
E X C I T E D E M
```

226

Feeling Words

Word Bank

afraid	funny	happy
sad	sleepy	tired

Directions: Use the words in the Word Bank to write the correct feeling word in each sentence.

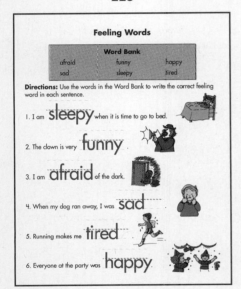

1. I am **sleepy** when it is time to go to bed.

2. The clown is very **funny**

3. I am **afraid** of the dark.

4. When my dog ran away, I was **sad**

5. Running makes me **tired**

6. Everyone at the party was **happy**

227

Feeling Words

Directions: Use the words in the Word Bank to write the correct feeling word under each story.

Word Bank

happy	excited	sad	mad

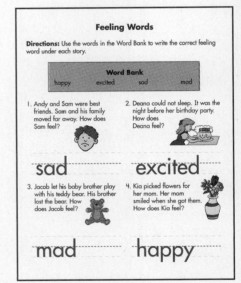

1. Andy and Sam were best friends. Sam and his family moved far away. How does Sam feel?

2. Deana could not sleep. It was the night before her birthday party. How does Deana feel?

sad   **excited**

3. Jacob let his baby brother play with his teddy bear. His brother lost the bear. How does Jacob feel?

4. Kia picked flowers for her mom. Her mom smiled when she got them. How does Kia feel?

mad   **happy**

228

Unit 9 Review

Directions: Use the words in the Word Bank to write three examples of each kind of word.

Word Bank

sad	they	no/know	Monday	fall	smell
sea/see	Miss	silly	hear	Thursday	right/write
cross	touch	pleased	land	you	Saturday

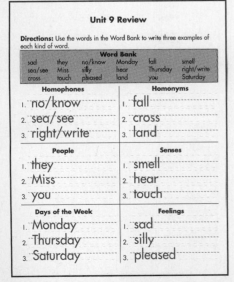

Homophones
1. no/know
2. sea/see
3. right/write

Homonyms
1. fall
2. cross
3. land

People
1. they
2. Miss
3. you

Senses
1. smell
2. hear
3. touch

Days of the Week
1. Monday
2. Thursday
3. Saturday

Feelings
1. sad
2. silly
3. pleased

229

Commonly Misused Words

The word **can** means **am able to** or **to be able to**.
Examples: I **can** do that for you.
Can you do that for me?

The word **may** means **be allowed to** or **permitted to**. **May** is used to ask or to give permission. **May** can also mean **might** or **perhaps**.
Examples: **May** I be excused?
You **may** sit here.

Directions: Write **can** or **may** to complete each sentence. The first one is done for you.

1. **May** Can/May I help you?
2. **can** He's smart. He can/may do it himself.
3. **may** When can/may I have my dessert?
4. **can** He can/may speak French fluently.
5. **may** You can/may use my pencil.
6. **May** Can/May my friend stay for dinner?
7. **may** You can/may leave when your report is finished.
8. **Can** Can/May you hear the dog barking?

231

Commonly Misused Words

The word **sit** means **to rest**.
Examples: Please **sit** here!
Will you **sit** by me?

The word **set** means **to put** or **place something**.
Examples: **Set** your purse there.
Set the dishes on the table.

Directions: Write **sit** or **set** to complete each sentence. The first one is done for you.

1. sit — Would you please sit/set down here?
2. set — You can sit/set the groceries there.
3. sit — She is a person who cannot sit/set still.
4. set — Where did you sit/set your new shoes?
5. sit — They decided to sit/set together during the movie.
6. set — He sit/set the greasy pan in the sink.
7. set — She sit/set the candles on the cake.
8. set — Get ready! Get sit/set! Go!

232

Commonly Misused Words

The word **they're** means **they are**.
Examples: **They're** our very best friends!
Ask them if **they're** coming over tomorrow.

The word **their** shows ownership.
Examples: **Their** dog is friendly.
It is **their** bicycle.

The word **there** shows place or direction.
Examples: Look over **there**.
There it is!

Directions: Write **they're**, **their**, or **there** to complete each sentence. The first one is done for you.

1. There — They're/Their/There is the sweater I want!
2. their — Do you believe they're/their/there stories?
3. there — Be they're/their/there by one o'clock.
4. their — Have you met they're/their/there mother?
5. their — Do you like they're/their/there new car?
6. They're — They're/Their/There friendly to everyone.
7. they're — Did she say they're/their/there ready to go?
8. there — Is anyone they're/their/there?

233

People Words

Directions: Trace and write the word. Complete each sentence with the word. Then, draw a picture of how you play.

play **play**   play

I can **play**

I like to **play**

How do I **play** ?

Pictures
will vary.

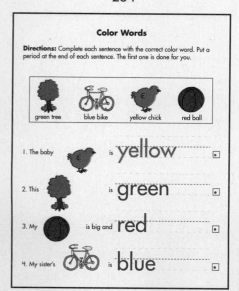

234

Color Words

Directions: Trace and write the color words. The first one is done for you.

orange   orange

blue   blue

green   green

yellow   yellow

red   red

brown   brown

235

Color Words

Directions: Complete each sentence with the correct color word. Put a period at the end of each sentence. The first one is done for you.

green tree   blue bike   yellow chick   red ball

1. The baby ___ is **yellow**.

2. This ___ is **green**.

3. My ___ is big and **red**.

4. My sister's ___ is **blue**.

236

Color Words

Directions: Complete the puzzle about colors.

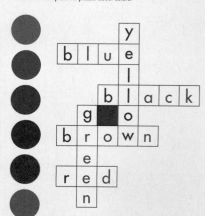

237

340

Time Words

The months of the year begin with capital letters.

Directions: Use the words in the Word Bank to write the months of the year in order on the calendar.

Word Bank

January	December	April	May	October	June
September	February	July	March	November	August

January		July	
February		August	
March		September	
April		October	
May		November	
June		December	

238

Commonly Misused Words

Use the word **good** to describe a person, place, or thing.

Example: He is a **good** teacher.

Use the word **well** to describe how something is done or how someone is feeling.

Example: She is not feeling **well**.

Directions: Trace and write the commonly misused words. Then, complete each sentence with the correct word.

good   good

well   well

1. I can throw the ball **well**

2. She is **good** at drawing.

239

Commonly Misused Words

Here is Sue. She is a **good** skater. She skates **well**.

When you describe a person, a place, or a thing, use the word **good**. When you describe how something is done, use the word **well**.

Directions: Circle **good** or **well** to complete each sentence.

1. Andrew is a (good) well singer.

2. Wanda dances good (well).

3. Antonio writes stories good (well).

4. Tim is a (good) well reader.

5. Carmen is a (good) well cook.

6. Helen paints good (well).

7. Doug adds numbers good (well).

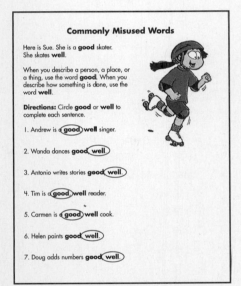

240

Commonly Misused Words

The word **its** shows ownership.
Example: **Its** leaves are green.

The word **it's** means **it is**.
Example: **It's** better to be early than late.

Directions: Trace and write the commonly misused words. Then, complete each sentence with the correct word.

its   its

it's   it's

1. The cat is licking **its** paws.

2. **It's** a beautiful day outside.

241

People Words

Directions: Trace and write the word. Complete each sentence with the word. Then, draw a picture of how you work.

work   **work**   **work**

I can **work**

I like to **work**

How do I **work** ?

Pictures will vary.

242

Color Words

Directions: Write three sentences that tell about this picture. Use a color word in each one. Begin each sentence with a capital letter and end it with a period.

1. Sentences will vary.

2.

3.

243

Color Words

Directions: Use the words in the Word Bank to complete each sentence with the correct color word.

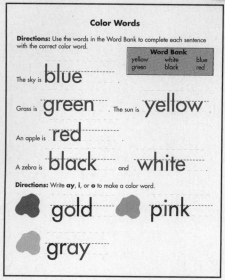

Word Bank
yellow   white   blue
green   black   red

The sky is **blue**

Grass is **green** . The sun is **yellow**

An apple is **red**

A zebra is **black** and **white**

Directions: Write **ay, i,** or **o** to make a color word.

gold   **pink**

gray

244

Color Words

Directions: Use the words in the Word Bank to complete the puzzles about colors.

Across
1. A ___ is ___

Down
2. An ___ is ___

o r a n g e
   e
   d

g
purple
r
a
y

Across
2. A ___ are ___

Down
1. An ___ is ___

Across
2. A ___ is ___

Down
1. A ___ is ___

b
green
o
w
n

Word Bank
brown   orange   purple   green   red   gray

245

Time Words

There are 12 months in a year. The first month is January. The last month is December. Some months have 31 days. Some months have 30 days. February is the shortest month with 28 days.

Directions: Write 1 to 12 in the boxes to put the months in order. The first one is done for you.

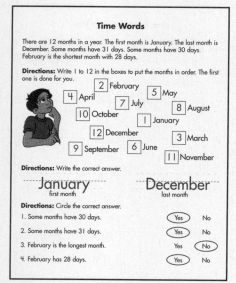

[2] February   [5] May
[4] April   [7] July   [8] August
[10] October   [1] January
[12] December   [3] March
[9] September   [6] June
[11] November

Directions: Write the correct answer.

January
first month

December
last month

Directions: Circle the correct answer.

1. Some months have 30 days.   (Yes)   No
2. Some months have 31 days.   (Yes)   No
3. February is the longest month.   Yes   (No)
4. February has 28 days.   (Yes)   No

246

Commonly Misused Words

The word **this** is a describing word that refers to things that are near. **This** always describes a single person, place, or thing.
Example: I will buy **this** coat.

The word **these** is also a describing word that refers to things that are near. **These** always describes more than one person, place, or thing.
Example: I will buy **these** flowers.

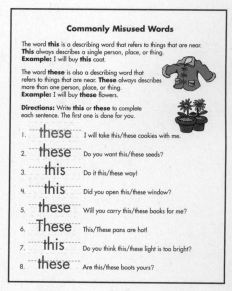

Directions: Write **this** or **these** to complete each sentence. The first one is done for you.

1. **these**   I will take this/these cookies with me.
2. **these**   Do you want this/these seeds?
3. **this**   Do it this/these way!
4. **this**   Did you open this/these window?
5. **these**   Will you carry this/these books for me?
6. **These**   This/These pans are hot!
7. **this**   Do you think this/these light is too bright?
8. **these**   Are this/these boots yours?

247

Commonly Misused Words

The word **your** shows possession.
Examples: Is that **your** book?
I visited **your** class.

The word **you're** means **you are.**
Examples: **You're** doing well on that painting.
If **you're** going to pass the test, you should study.

Directions: Write **your** or **you're** to complete each sentence. The first one is done for you.

1. **You're**   Your/You're the best friend I have!
2. **Your**   Your/You're brother came to see me.
3. **you're**   If your/you're going, you'd better hurry!
4. **your**   It's none of your/you're business!
5. **You're**   Your/You're kidding!
6. **your**   I thought your/you're report was great!
7. **you're**   He thinks your/you're wonderful!
8. **your**   What is your/you're first choice?

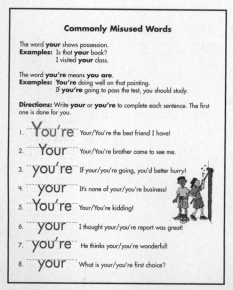

248

Commonly Misused Words

Directions: Help the coach get to the castle. Complete each sentence with the correct word.

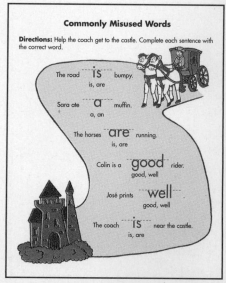

The road **is** bumpy.
is, are

Sara ate **a** muffin.
a, an

The horses **are** running.
is, are

Colin is a **good** rider.
good, well

José prints **well**
good, well

The coach **is** near the castle.
is, are

249

People Words

Directions: List at least 15 different kinds of people you might see while out on a walk. Go on a walk with an adult. When you spot people you listed, check them off of your list. Some suggestions are: police officer, truck driver, jogger, etc.

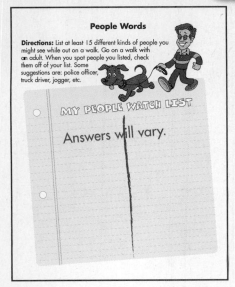

MY PEOPLE WATCH LIST

Answers will vary.

250

Color Words

Directions: Use the words in the Word Bank to find the color words. Look up, down, and sideways.

o	r	a	n	g	e	b	d	c	a	e	g	i	k	r	z	t
p	x	h	o	e	b	u	n	w	n	f	a	d	f	e	q	x
i	l	m	n	b	l	v	c	x	z	a	s	f	g	d	h	a
n	y	u	i	o	u	r	e	w	q	t	p	w	h	i	t	e
k	g	r	a	y	e	x	p	b	n	v	m	x	k	y	u	p
b	u	d	r	u	g	t	u	b	r	o	w	n	m	e	n	o
l	a	s	d	m	r	r	r	v	n	e	t	y	w	l	l	h
a	b	d	f	g	e	h	p	j	k	m	u	z	m	l	n	e
c	g	h	k	o	e	i	l	e	w	n	l	v	f	o	g	n
k	s	d	u	e	n	l	e	j	o	m	c	s	x	w	y	w

Word Bank

blue	black	brown
yellow	red	pink
orange	gray	green
purple	white	

Color the squares you circled blue. What did you find? Art

251

Spanish Color Words

Directions: Use the words in the Word Bank to write the color words in Spanish on the rainbow. Then, color the rainbow.

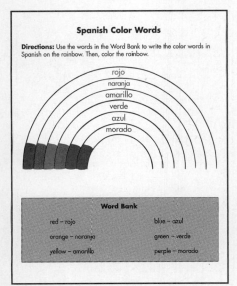

rojo
naranja
amarillo
verde
azul
morado

Word Bank

red – rojo	blue – azul
orange – naranja	green – verde
yellow – amarillo	purple – morado

252

Spanish Color Words

- red – rojo (rō–hō)
- orange – naranja (nah–rahn–ha)
- yellow – amarillo (ah–mah–rē–yō)
- green – verde (ver–dā)
- blue – azul (ah–zool)
- purple – morado (mō–rah–dō)
- black – negro (nā–grō)
- white – blanco (blāhn–kō)
- brown – marrón (mah–rōn)

Directions: Read each color word. Say each color word in Spanish. Then, write the Spanish word next to the English word. Color each crayon to match the color word.

black	negro		red	rojo
blue	azul		purple	morado
green	verde		white	blanco
brown	morrón		yellow	amarillo
orange	naranja			

253

Unit 10 Review

Directions: Circle the correct word for each sentence. Write it on the line.

1. He is a **good** student. (good) well

2. **It's** hard to sit still when it is sunny outside. Its (It's)

3. Is she **your** sister? (your) you're

4. You may **set** your book bag on the table. sit (set)

5. I like to visit **their** house. (their) there

6. **February** is the shortest month. May (February)

Directions: Read each color word. Then, circle the two things that the color word describes.

1. azul — (sky) cow (water)
2. naranja — (carrot) (pumpkin) grapes
3. verde — (leaf) elephant (grass)
4. amarillo — (sun) horse (lemon)

254

Words You Use Often

Directions: Trace and write the commonly used words.

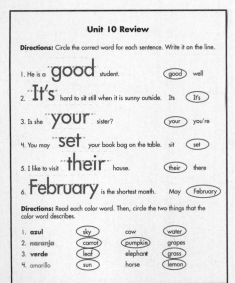

the — the
are — are
for — for
was — was
said — said
you — you

256

Words You Use Often

Directions: Use the words in the Word Bank to complete the story.

Word Bank					
You	for	was	said	the	are

I **was** late for **the** party!

" **You** must hurry," **said** my mom.

Your friends **are** waiting **for** you.

Directions: A **contraction** is two words joined into one shorter word. Use the words in the Word Bank to write the correct contraction on each line.

Word Bank
are not = aren't
was not = wasn't
you are = you're

was not   you are   are not

wasn't you're aren't

257

Words You Use Often

Directions: Draw a line to match the beginning letter of each word with the rest of its letters.

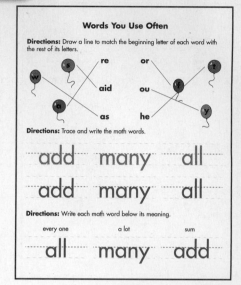

Directions: Trace and write the math words.

add   many   all

add   many   all

Directions: Write each math word below its meaning.

every one   a lot   sum

all   many   add

258

Job Words

Directions: Use the words in the Word Bank to complete each sentence with the correct job word.

Word Bank		
pilot	farmer	doctor
builder	plumber	teacher

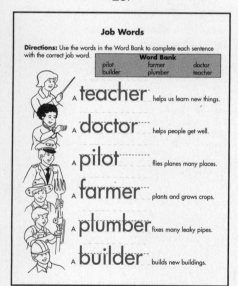

A **teacher** helps us learn new things.

A **doctor** helps people get well.

A **pilot** flies planes many places.

A **farmer** plants and grows crops.

A **plumber** fixes many leaky pipes.

A **builder** builds new buildings.

259

Magnet Words

A magnet can **pull** another magnet. Or a magnet can **push** another magnet.

Directions: Trace and write the magnet words.

pull   **pull   pull**

push   **push   push**

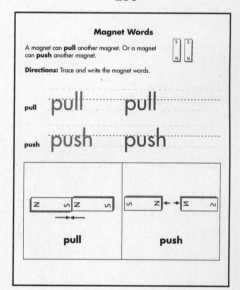

pull   push

260

Magnet Words

Every magnet has a north pole and a south pole.

When a north pole and a south pole are next to each other, they **pull** together.

S		N		S		N

When two north poles or two south poles are next to each other, they **push** apart.

S		N		N		S

Directions: Write **push** or **pull** to tell what each pair of magnets will do.

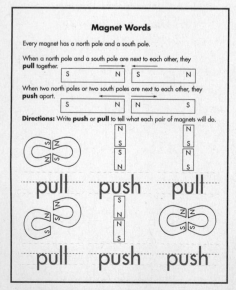

pull   push   pull

pull   push   push

261

Magnet Words

Directions: Trace and write the words. Then, make lists of the things in your bedroom that will and will not stick to a magnet. (Do not try your magnet on anything electronic.)

magnet   **magnet magnet**

Magnets stick to:	Magnets do not stick to:
Lists will vary.	

262

Money Words

Directions: Read about coins. Then, answer the questions.

You can use coins to buy things. Some coins are worth more than others. Do you know these coins? A penny is worth one cent. A nickel is worth five cents. A dime is worth 10 cents. A quarter is worth 25 cents.

1. What can you use coins to do?

You can use coins to buy things.

2. How are coins different?

Some coins are worth more than others.

Directions: Number the coins in order from the one that is worth the least to the one that is worth the most. Then, write how many cents each coin is worth.

 nickel **2**   penny **1**   dime **3**

5 cents   **1** cent   **10** cents

263

Words You Use Often

Directions: Use the words in the Word Bank to write about a time when you had to count things.

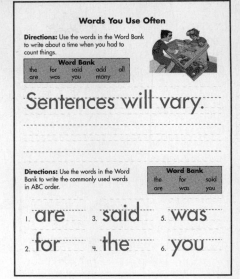

Word Bank

the	for	said	add	all
are	was	you	many	

Sentences will vary.

Directions: Use the words in the Word Bank to write the commonly used words in ABC order.

Word Bank

the	for	said
are	was	you

1. **are**   3. **said**   5. **was**

2. **for**   4. **the**   6. **you**

264

Words You Use Often

Directions: Trace and write the commonly used words.

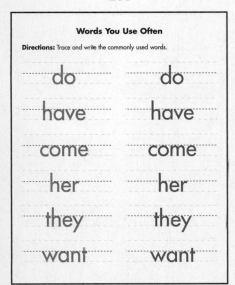

do   do

have   have

come   come

her   her

they   they

want   want

265

Words You Use Often

Directions: Use the words in the Word Bank to complete each sentence with the correct commonly used word.

Word Bank

her	come	want	do	have	they

I **have** two friends who **want**

to play. I'll ask Mom if I need to **do** some work

first. Then, I'll ask **her** if **they**

can **come** over.

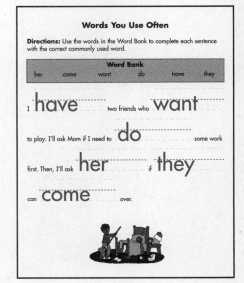

266

Job Words

Directions: Use the words in the Word Bank to complete the puzzle about jobs.

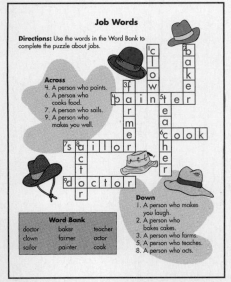

Across
4. A person who paints.
6. A person who cooks food.
7. A person who sails.
9. A person who makes you well.

Down
1. A person who makes you laugh.
2. A person who bakes cakes.
3. A person who farms.
5. A person who teaches.
8. A person who acts.

Crossword answers: clown, baker, painter, farmer, teacher, cook, sailor, actor, doctor

Word Bank

doctor	baker	teacher
clown	farmer	actor
sailor	painter	cook

267

Words About Simple Machines

A **lever** is a simple machine used to lift or move things. It has two parts. The **arm** is the part that moves. The **fulcrum** supports the arm but does not move.

Directions: Label the parts of this lever.

arm

fulcrum

Directions: The letters in each word are mixed up. Unscramble the letters to write the name of each kind of lever correctly.

velosh → **shovel**

mrahem → **hammer**

orbom → **broom**

tun reckarc → **nut cracker**

268

Words About Simple Machines

Directions: Use the words in the Word Bank to name the simple machine in each picture. Then, you will find the answer to this question: What do machines use to work?

1. whe**e**l and axle
2. inclin**e**d plane
3. l**e**ver
4. s c r **e** w
5. wed**g**e
6. p u l l e **y**

Word Bank

wheel and axle	inclined plane	screw
wedge	lever	pulley

269

Words About Simple Machines

Directions: Use the words in the Word Bank to write the correct tools under each simple machine.

Inclined Plane
truck ramp
sloped sidewalk
slide

Wheel and Axle
car
mixer
skateboard
light switch

Lever
bottle opener
shovel

Wedge
ax
doorstop
screwdriver

Word Bank

car	mixer	light switch
ax	screwdriver	doorstop
skateboard	shovel	truck ramp
sloped sidewalk	slide	bottle opener

270

Words About Fractions

The word **equal** means **the same**. The word **unequal** means **not the same**.

Directions: Circle each shape that is divided into equal parts. Draw an **X** on each shape that is divided into unequal parts.

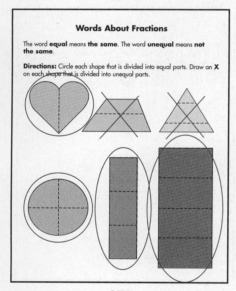

271

Words You Use Often

Directions: Use the words in the Word Bank to find the commonly used words. Look up, down, and sideways.

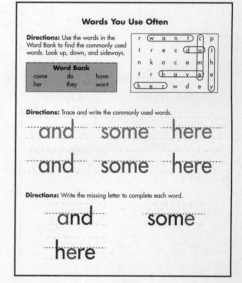

Word Bank

come	do	have
her	they	want

Directions: Trace and write the commonly used words.

and   some   here

and   some   here

Directions: Write the missing letter to complete each word.

and   some

here

272

Words You Use Often

Directions: Do you like people to visit you at home? Use the words in the Word Bank to write about your favorite visitors.

Word Bank

do	come	they	and	here
have	her	want	some	

Sentences will vary.

Directions: Circle the word in each pair that is not spelled correctly.

1. they (thay)   4. (cume) come
2. (dou) do   5. (hur) her
3. have (hav)   6. want (wonte)

273

Overused Words

It is easy to use certain words again and again. Try giving "tired" words a break!

Directions: Use the words in the Word Bank to replace the tired words in the paragraph. Rewrite the paragraph.

Word Bank

gorgeous	pleasant	friendly	countless

Last Friday, our class had a <u>nice</u> time at the Tropical Gardens. We saw <u>many</u> flowers, trees, and plants. The exotic birds were <u>beautiful</u>. We had a <u>good</u> guide who let us take pictures.

nice—pleasant
many—countless
beautiful—gorgeous
good—friendly

274

Job Words

Directions: Draw a picture of what you might look like when you grow up. Then, write what you want to be when you grow up.

When I grow up, I want to be a

Answers will vary.

because . . .

Pictures will vary.

275

Words About Simple Machines

Directions: Tyrone and Kim have a list of jobs to do. Help them pick the right tool for each job. Draw a line from each job to the correct tool.

1. What will help Kim raise the flag up the flagpole? — inclined plane
2. What will Tyrone use to help him get the cat out of the tree? — pulley
3. What will Kim use to carry sand to her new sandbox? — lever
4. What will Tyrone use to get the nail out of the board? — screw
5. What will Kim use to hang the mirror on her bedroom door? — wheel and axle
6. What will Tyrone use to slice the turkey? — wedge

276

Words About Simple Machines

Directions: Color and cut out each simple machine. Then, glue each one in the correct place.

Screw	Lever	Pulley
Wedge	Wheel and Axle	Inclined Plane

Goes with wheel and axle
Goes with lever
Goes with inclined plane
Goes with wedge
Goes with screw
Goes with pulley

277

Unit 11 Review

Directions: An inventor is a person who invents or makes new things. Pretend that you are an inventor. Draw a simple machine. Then, write two sentences to explain how your machine works.

Pictures will vary.

Sentences will vary.

279

Story Words

Story elements are the parts of a story that make up its beginning, middle, and end. A good story will contain these story elements:

Title — the name of a story that gives a clue as to what the story is about
Setting — where and when the story takes place
Characters — the people, animals, or objects that the story is about
Plot — the sequence of events in a story that create a problem
Climax — the most thrilling part of the story where the problem is either solved or the plot thickens
Resolution — how the characters solve the story problem
Conclusion — what happens to the characters in the end

Directions: Write the letter of the definition that matches the story element.

1. d Setting — a. the way a story ends
2. e Characters — b. the changing point of a story—often the most exciting part of the story
3. c Plot — c. the series of events in a story involving a problem
4. b Climax — d. the place and time
5. f Resolution — e. people or animals in the story
6. a Conclusion — f. the way in which the problems are solved

281

Story Words

A **character** is the **person**, **animal**, or **object** that a story is about. You can't have a story without a character.

Characters are usually people, but sometimes they are animals, aliens, or even objects that come to life. You can have many characters in a story.

Directions: Read the story. Circle the three characters named in the story.

Rorie the Reader!

Rorie loved to read. Rorie would read everything she could find: books, magazines, even cereal boxes!

She loved to read so much that she would always carry books in her bag in case she had a free second to read.

Rorie had blond hair and was very pale. Her mom would say, "Rorie, please go outside and play. You need to get some sunshine."

Rorie would answer, "Do I have to, Mom? I would rather read."

One day, Rorie's teacher said to her mom, "I have never seen a girl who loves to read so much. You are very lucky to have a daughter like Rorie." From then on, Rorie's mom let her read whenever she wanted.

282

Story Words

The **events** in a story describe all the things that happen.

Directions: Read each problem. Write two events that tell what happens.

1. Heavy black clouds darken the sky. Travis is walking home without an umbrella.
   Answers will vary.

2. Marcella worked very hard on her book report last night. This morning, she was in such a rush to get to school that she left her report on the table at home.
   Answers will vary.

3. Ben's school is having a fundraiser. In order to win the scooter, Ben will have to sell 50 magazine subscriptions.
   Answers will vary.

283

Clothing Words

Directions: Trace and write the clothing words. The first one is done for you.

shirt   shirt
pants   pants
jacket   jacket
socks   socks
shoes   shoes
dress   dress
hat   hat

284

Words About Things That Go

Directions: Trace and write the names of the things that go. Then, color the pictures. The first one is done for you.

Color the pictures.

 car   car

 truck   truck

 train   train

 bike   bike

 plane   plane

285

Words About Things That Go

Directions: Write the missing letter or letters for each word. The first one is done for you.

 car   car

 plane   plane

 bike   bike

 train   train

 truck   truck

286

Words About Things That Go

Directions: The letters in each word are mixed up. Unscramble the letters to write each word correctly. The first one is done for you.

 rac   car

 aitrn   train

 eplna   plane

 kibe   bike

 ckutr   truck

287

Weight Words

Directions: Read about weight. Then, circle the correct answers.

Weight is a measurement that tells how heavy something is. Almost everything in your room can be weighed.

You can describe weight in **pounds** or **ounces**. You can describe weight in **kilograms** or **grams**.

Where have you seen weight? Maybe you have seen weight on a box of cereal. Food is sometimes weighed in **ounces** or **grams**. Maybe the nurse weighed you at the doctor's office. People often measure their own weight in **pounds** or **kilograms**.

1. Weight tells how _____ something is.
   a. long
   b. wide
   c. heavy

2. Which can be used to show weight?
   a. meters
   b. grams
   c. liters

3. How are people usually weighed?
   a. miles
   b. gallons
   c. pounds

4. How is food sometimes weighed?
   a. ounces
   b. meters
   c. inches

288

348

Story Words

Stories have a setting and a plot. The **setting** tells where and when the story takes place. The **plot** tells what happened.

Directions: Trace and write the story words. Then, complete each sentence with the correct story word.

setting **setting   setting**

plot **plot   plot**

Michael, Sam and Dominic were best friends. They ate lunch together. At recess, they swung on the swings together. On the swings, Michael said, "Come to my house to play after school." Dominic thought Michael was looking at Sam. He waited for Michael to ask him, too, but Michael didn't. All afternoon, Dominic felt sad. When the bell rang, he started to go home.
"Where are you going?" Michael called. "I wanted you both to come to my house." With a big smile, Dominic ran to join Michael and Sam.

1. In the story's **plot**, Michael invited his friends to play.

2. The jungle gym is the **setting** for the story.

289

Story Words

Every story has a setting. The **setting** is the place where the story happens.

Directions: Think of a place that you know well. It could be your room, your kitchen, your backyard, your classroom, or an imaginary place. Think about what you see, hear, smell, taste, or feel in that place. Brainstorm some words and ideas that describe the place. Write your ideas below.

Answers will vary.

290

Story Words

The **setting** is the place where the story happens. The setting is also the time when the story happens. Does it take place at night? On a sunny day? In the future? During the winter?

Time can be: time of day
a holiday
a season of the year
a time in history
a time in the future

Directions: Read the story. Then, answer the questions.

Pizza Night!

Last Tuesday, we made pizzas for dinner. We made mini-pizzas out of pita bread, tomato sauce, mozzarella cheese, and vegetable toppings. Then, my mom put our "M.P.s" (mini-pizzas) into the oven for the cheese to melt. Mmm-m-m! Delicious!

1. What time of day did this story take place? **dinner time /evening**

2. What day of the week did this story take place? **Tuesday**

3. What happened in the story? **The family made mini-pizzas for dinner.**

291

Clothing Words

Directions: The words by each picture are mixed up. Use them to write a sentence that tells about the picture. Begin each sentence with a capital letter and end it with a period.

Example: is shirt a drying.

A shirt is drying.

1. ties his shoes he

He ties his shoes.

2. red wear I a jacket

I wear a red jacket.

3. blue are pants his

His pants are blue.

292

Words About Things That Go

Directions: These sentences tell about things that go. Complete each sentence with the correct word. Use the pictures to help you.

Example:

The **car** is in the garage.

1. The **truck** was at the farm.

2. My **bike** had a flat tire.

3. The **plane** flew high.

4. The **train** went fast.

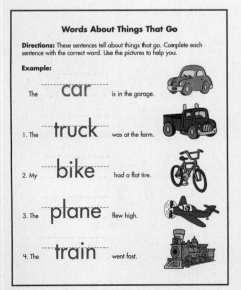

293

Words About Things That Go

Directions: Complete the names of the things that go. Then, draw a line from the first part of the sentence to the part that completes it. Put a period at the end of each sentence.

Example:

The blue **bike**   is in the bike rack ⊡

1. The **car**   carries dirt ⊡

2. Bob's **truck**   is purple ⊡

3. The **train**   flies high ⊡

4. My dad's **plane**   is full ⊡

294

Words About Things That Go

Directions: Draw a line from the first part of the sentence to the part that completes it. Put a period at the end of each sentence. The first one is done for you.

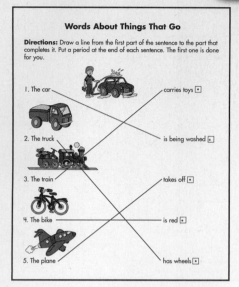

1. The car — carries toys ⊡
2. The truck — is being washed ⊡
3. The train — takes off ⊡
4. The bike — is red ⊡
5. The plane — has wheels ⊡

295

Weight Words

Directions: Read each question. Then, circle the correct answer.

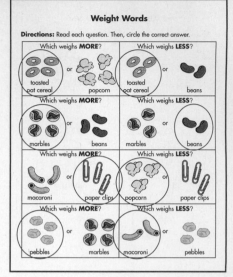

Which weighs **MORE**? — toasted oat cereal (or) popcorn
Which weighs **LESS**? — toasted oat cereal (or) beans
Which weighs **MORE**? — marbles (or) beans
Which weighs **LESS**? — marbles (or) beans
Which weighs **MORE**? — macaroni (or) paper clips
Which weighs **LESS**? — popcorn (or) paper clips
Which weighs **MORE**? — pebbles (or) marbles
Which weighs **LESS**? — macaroni (or) pebbles

296

Story Words

The **solution** in a story is the way the problem is solved. Sometimes, the main character solves the problem. Sometimes, the problem is solved in other ways.

Directions: Draw a line from each story to its solution.

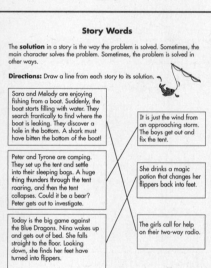

Sara and Melody are enjoying fishing from a boat. Suddenly, the boat starts filling with water. They search frantically to find where the boat is leaking. They discover a hole in the bottom. A shark must have bitten the bottom of the boat!

It is just the wind from an approaching storm. The boys get out and fix the tent.

Peter and Tyrone are camping. They set up the tent and settle into their sleeping bags. A huge thing thunders through the tent roaring, and then the tent collapses. Could it be a bear? Peter gets out to investigate.

She drinks a magic potion that changes her flippers back into feet.

Today is the big game against the Blue Dragons. Nina wakes up and gets out of bed. She falls straight to the floor. Looking down, she finds her feet have turned into flippers.

The girls call for help on their two-way radio.

297

Story Words

In some paragraphs, the order of the sentences is very important. **Transition words**, such as **first**, **next**, **after**, **then**, **finally**, and **last**, offer clues to help show the sequence of the sentences.

Directions: Read the story. Circle the transition words.

My brother is convinced that he makes the best apple pie in the world! He claims he has tried over 100 different recipes and has found the perfect one.

(First,) he says it's all about the apples. He is convinced you must use only hand-picked Granny Smith apples. (Next,) you must carefully slice all the apples. (After) you have sliced them, you must add white and brown sugar, nutmeg, lemon juice, and butter. (Then,) you need to preheat the oven while you make the crust.

(Finally,) when the crust is ready, you put the apples in the crust and bake it at 350 degrees for a perfect apple pie!

298

Story Words

A **fiction** book is a book about things that are made up or not true. Fantasy books are fiction. A **nonfiction** book is about things that have really happened. Books can be classified into more types within these two groups.

Mystery – a book that has clues that lead to solving a problem or mystery
Biography – a book about a real person's life
Poetry – a book that has a collection of poems, which may or may not rhyme
Fantasy – a book about things that cannot really happen
Sports – a book about different sports or sports figures
Travel – a book about going to other places

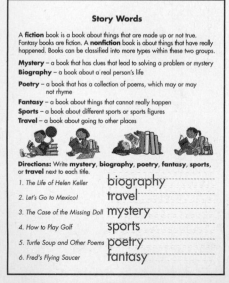

Directions: Write **mystery**, **biography**, **poetry**, **fantasy**, **sports**, or **travel** next to each title.

1. *The Life of Helen Keller*   biography
2. *Let's Go to Mexico!*   travel
3. *The Case of the Missing Doll*   mystery
4. *How to Play Golf*   sports
5. *Turtle Soup and Other Poems*   poetry
6. *Fred's Flying Saucer*   fantasy

299

Clothing Words

Directions: Complete each sentence with a clothing word. Use the pictures to help you. Put a period at the end of each sentence.

Example:
Mike is wearing a   hat ⊡

1. Put on your socks before your   shoes ⊡
2. When it's cold wear a   jacket ⊡
3. The little girl liked to wear a pink   dress ⊡
4. He wore jeans with the   shirt ⊡
5. The man wore a suit coat and   pants ⊡
6. The clown wore long, striped   socks ⊡

300

Words About Things That Go

Directions: Read the story.

Sarah built a car for a race. Sarah's car has wheels, a steering wheel, and a place to sit just like the family car. It doesn't have a motor, a key, or a gas pedal. Sarah came in second in last year's race. This year, she hopes to win the race.

Directions: Write **S** beside the things Sarah's car has that are like things the family car has. Write **D** beside the things that are different.

1. **S**   steering wheel
2. **D**   motor
3. **D**   gas pedal
4. **S**   seat
5. **S**   wheels

301

Words About Things That Go

Directions: Read about boats. Then, answer the questions.

See the boats! They float on water. Some boats have sails. The wind moves the sails. It makes the boats go. Many people name their sailboats. They paint the name on the side of the boat.

1. What makes sailboats move?   **wind**

2. Where do sailboats float?   **on water**

3. What would you name a sailboat?   **Answers will vary.**

302

Words About Things That Go

Directions: Find and circle the words from the Word Bank. Look across and down.

Word Bank

monorail	trains	cable cars	schoolbus	tram
airplane	bus	elevator	ship	truck
boat	cab	escalator	subway	van
car	jet	helicopter	taxi	

s	g	a	b	g	t	h	o	v	i	w	a	k	l	o	h
f	t	r	u	c	k	e	l	e	v	a	t	o	r	n	e
s	s	h	i	p	e	s	c	a	l	a	t	o	r	b	c
u	b	o	a	t	c	a	b	l	e	c	a	r	s	h	w
p	t	a	x	i	s	c	h	o	o	l	b	u	s	e	g
x	t	r	a	i	n	s	a	i	r	p	l	a	n	e	y
o	t	r	a	m	h	e	l	i	c	o	p	t	e	r	a
f	s	u	b	w	a	y	m	o	n	o	r	a	i	l	l
n	o	s	b	u	s	o	e	f	a	c	a	b	p	c	r
y	n	e	c	a	r	u	n	f	t	j	e	t	o	i	e

Color the squares you circled yellow.

What did you find?   **bus**

303

Unit 12 Review

Directions: Write a story about a place that you would like to visit. Think about:
- How you will get there.
- What you will wear.
- Who you will see.
- What will happen while you are there.

resolution   **plane**   then

car   travel   characters   **plot**   jacket   climax

Stories will vary.

finally   **hat**   **see**   setting   conclusion   next   **bike**

304

Notes